A Year at the Catholic Worker

A Year at the Catholic Worker

A Spiritual Journey Among the Poor

by

Marc H. Ellis

Baylor University Press
Waco, Texas

to my family

to those who seek
to those who serve

An earlier version of this work was published under the title *A Year at the Catholic Worker* by Paulist Press, 1978.

ISBN: 0-918954-74-6

Printed in the United States of America on acid-free paper.

Contents

Editor's Note

With this edition of Marc Ellis's *A Year at the Catholic Worker*, the Baylor University Press inaugurates a new series, "Literature and the Religious Spirit," intended to return to print important literary works of fiction, creative nonfiction, and spiritual autobiography by writers of faith. It is the fate of most literary works these days, both great and small, to eventually disappear from bookstore shelves; the result, of course, is that eventually even works by major writers and thinkers are effectively lost to critics, students, and the general reading public. But by reprinting such works, the Baylor University Press hopes to acquaint a new generation of readers with significant works of literature by major writers. Our editions are intended to be both bookstore- and classroom-friendly; each book will add to an authoritative text an introduction, an interview or interviews with the author, and a short bibliography of primary and secondary works to acquaint a new reader with the author's canon and major critical responses to it.

A Year at the Catholic Worker is an ideal book to launch "Literature and the Religious Spirit": the work was uniformly acclaimed when first published twenty-five years ago; it expertly recounts an important epoch in contemporary Christian social history; and of course, most importantly, it traces important episodes in the development of the thought and social conscience of a major twentieth-century thinker. Marc Ellis has gone on from the writing of *A Year at the Catholic Worker* to become a significant voice in the post-Holocaust Jewish/Christian dialogue. He speaks nationally and internationally on the issues which arise from the facts of the Holocaust and the establishment of a Jewish state, and his books—among them such works as *Ending Auschwitz: The Future of Jewish and Christian Life; Toward a Jewish Theology of Liberation; Unholy Alliance: Religion and Atrocity in Our Time; Beyond Innocence and Redemption: Confronting the Holocaust and Israeli Power;* and the recent *O, Jerusalem!: The Contested Future of the Jewish Covenant*—challenge Jews and Christians alike to rethink past and present atrocities and to live justly for the future. That Marc Ellis is now a member of the Baylor University faculty only adds to our excitement in launching "Literature and the Religious Spirit" with his first book. We hope you will find it stimulating reading and will look forward to future books in the series.

Greg Garrett, General Editor

Preface

The author of this book is quite correct in the division he has made of the existing literature devoted to the Catholic Worker movement: books by sympathetic, intellectual observers, of one sort or another, or books by those whose entire lives have been very much part of a particular social and religious effort. His book provides, as he points out, a third alternative—and an important one. He is young—and so with a perspective of a new generation. The Catholic Worker movement is approaching its half century of life, and inevitably, its meaning must be assessed by the men and women of Marc Ellis' generation as well as by those of us whose hair is greying; or is all white. He is Jewish—an outsider by ancestry to an experiment in action and faith that is, obviously, Catholic in its inspiring commitment. And he is honest, decent, thoughtful, sensitive, and clear-headed—as well as a strong, lucid writer; and so, his observations, inevitably and properly, will influence, even persuade the readers who come upon this book.

I hope there will be many of them—men and women from all over this country who will be lucky, indeed, to find their way to this modest, touching, reflective journal, kept by a youth who knows his Dostoevsky (one of Dorothy Day's favorite novelists) and who has in his soul a touch of the unashamed,

2

surprising, simple spirituality that passionate Russian pilgrim so repeatedly evoked in his various stories. Moreover, Marc Ellis' religious inclinations and ideals, like those of the characters in, say, *The Brothers Karamazov* and *The Idiot*, serve to affect others deeply—and inform anyone with half an interest in thinking about life, in understanding its meaning. One goes through the pages of this book and meets very special people, gets to know their purposes, their hopes and struggles, their failures and small but significant triumphs. The Catholic Worker movement can be approached through resort to the abstract, through theological and philosophical and political analysis; but it has been, really, a movement of lives—of men and women who have tried for various lengths of time to serve God and his principles, as they have come down to us in the Old and New Testaments. Those lives, some of them, are given to us here—as seen and heard by a visitor at 36 East First Street, who stayed a year, and maybe, will spend a lifetime under the spell of the experience.

We are not given arguments, a critique, a theoretical discussion. We are not provided one of those "contexts" that social scientists, these days, are so anxious to come up with. We are not offered explanations, justifications, repudiations, or sly evidence of someone's intellectual virtue. This book is a response of the heart and soul to a movement whose daily presence among us may be described as mysterious—hence not to be explained, but experienced with continuing awe and gratitude: God's grace at work in the various "acts" of sinful, flawed, humble people, his servants on this earth. One be-

3

gins to think, by the end of this book, that the writer—who would be the last one to make any claims for himself—belongs firmly in the company, will in one way or another stay in the company, of those Catholic Workers he chose to be with, and in these pages, manages to portray quietly, but vividly and with a convincing intelligence.

Robert Coles

Foreword

My first awareness of Marc came in February of 1974 when Dorothy Day, on one of her Catholic Worker pastoral tours, (as her innumerable bus trips amounted to) visited the family at Lloyd, Florida. At the time, I was teaching at Florida State University at Tallahassee, and when word got out that Dorothy was in town a petition was made that she speak to the students who knew of her and the Catholic Worker. So, reluctantly and with some groaning, because she was very tired, she talked, one afternoon, to a classroom full of students. When it was over, some of her auditors came up to (1) point out her lack of "realism" concerning the true nature of people, of communism, of the universe; (2) say "thank you, your talk was so inspiring"; (3) profess the stirring of a spirit-felt emotion that assented to what she said, but to wonder how in the world a college student caught in the necessity of charting the truth of the objective world could do anything but bow to the system.

I was in a hurry to get Dorothy out, but one student whom I knew vaguely as a religion major, lingered at the desk in earnest conversation with Dorothy, and I, standing aside, heard him say that while he did feel profoundly moved by Dorothy's vision of an essential human unity and her Gospel call to transform this unity into community by the practice of voluntary poverty, he wondered what

6

place he, according to the canons of higher learning, and, in a hot pursuit of an objective reality, could have in her world. Not wishing to listen in on a conversation that was becoming personal, I turned away, but I would guess what Dorothy told Marc was that he should feed the poor.

So that was the last I saw of Marc for a while. When summer came I had an opportunity to see Dorothy, who was staying at the Catholic Worker house at 36 East First Street, so I drove my Datsun to New York City in a rain-drenched trip and got to the First Street house shortly after noon. On the several occasions that I have been to the house, I have always entered with some mild trepidation, being concerned that I refrain from a demonstrative exercise of pious goodwill where the guests are concerned (all too easy to do when one plans to stay an hour or so) and, on the other hand, not be unnaturally reserved and wondering vaguely if one of those demented persons I saw outside might not come in and do me in.

Inside all was tranquil. A few guests sat at the tables drinking coffee and in the rear where there was an open kitchen area I saw a figure drying dishes. I looked and it dawned on me that it was Marc. "What are you doing here?" I asked, "Visiting, for several days or a week?" No, he had come to the Worker for an indefinite period.

"Marc," I said, "let's take a ride and talk about this." I wanted to explain to him that we all have our different callings and that living in the very heart of certain kinds of human wretchedness in a Catholic Worker house might be all right for a day or two but a sustained dose of it could be a harsh experience. Maybe he ought to come back to Florida State and pursue his quest at a more scholarly level.

But Marc stayed. After some time I got a letter from him, asking about the possibility of using his experience at the Worker house as a basis for an M.A. thesis in American Studies. The idea struck me as eminently sound, since what could be more authentic as a recreation of some significant aspect of American life than that in which one had personally participated? So after nine months at the St. Joseph Worker House, Marc returned to Florida State and portions of this journal of his days at the Worker were eventually accepted for his M.A. thesis.

Now this journal is to be published, and I am glad for two reasons. The first is that after thirty years of teaching I am increasingly convinced that the humanistic focus of higher education is becoming wildly blurred in what has become an accelerating pursuit of a so-called objective reality. Where is the heart and center of our humanness, to which we should be drawn, toward which we should be making our way to give hope and a sign of peace to the world? Assuredly, it is not to be found along the plunging, fragmenting course the world is pursuing and which an overworked apparatus of scholarship tries to interpret and guide. We must, once again, try to bring the object world into focus by reference to those prophetic statements of human meaning that humankind has received from those inspired by a vision of eternity and not of time.

Frequently I think of Peter Maurin, the founder of the Catholic Worker movement, trying to explain his radical vision of a person-centered creation to those gaunt and wordless men who sat on the benches of Union Square during the Depression

8

days. Maurin was the poor man who, in his poverty, is an object lesson for today's Church, and who, in his sense of the reality of the sacred, provides an instruction for today's teachers. And if these wordless men who sat on the Union Square benches wondered what Maurin was talking about, Dorothy Day eventually began to see, and the Catholic Worker movement has been the result. Marc, I know, understands Maurin and the radical redirection of the tendency of history that he bespoke. It is, therefore, a pleasure to see another person writing on a subject about which the world needs to know.

The second reason I am glad to see this journal published is that Marc is a Jew. It would have delighted Peter Maurin immeasurably to know that someone of the people of Israel had become a servant of the poor in one of the houses of hospitality that Peter had envisioned. Peter, as Dorothy Day has frequently said, had a special love for the Jews, and I have always thought that one of his most poetic and effective essays was his paraphrase of Leon Bloy:

We forget
   or rather
   we do not wish to know
   that Our Lord made man
   was a Jew,
   the Jew par excellence,
   the Lion of Judah;
   that his mother was a
     Jewess,
   the flower of the Jewish race,
   that his ancestors were Jews
   along with all the prophets,

finally that our whole
   sacred liturgy
is drawn from Jewish books.
How then can we express
   the enormity of the outrage
   and the blasphemy involved
   in vilifying the Jewish race . . .?
The history of the Jews
   dams the history
   of the human race
   as a dike
   dams a river
   in order
   to raise its level.

Yes, Peter would be pleased, the more so because Marc professes the source of his Jewishness in Abraham's covenant with God. Finding the meaning for his existence in the desert experience of his forefathers, Marc doubtless believes that he has given added richness to this experience by serving the poor at a Catholic Worker house of hospitality. For me I choose to see his action as a sign, almost prophetic, of the true spirit of Israel.

Finally, it is significant that the Paulist Press is publishing Marc's journal, for it was the Paulist Press that printed the first editions of the *Catholic Worker*. Marc has told of his days at the Worker with a literary quality that is his gift and which includes the virtue of simple directness. One expects more from him in the days to come.

William D. Miller
Marquette University
March 14, 1978

Introduction

Forty-five years ago the Catholic Worker movement began with the opening of a shared apartment as a house of hospitality, and the selling of the
Catholic Worker newspaper for a penny a copy in
Union Square. It began amidst the great depression
with millions out of work and the foundations of
American capitalism crumbling. Most of all, however, the Catholic Worker began with the meeting
of two persons: Dorothy Day and Peter Maurin.
Their meeting was the effective beginning of the
Catholic Worker movement and remains to this day
the source of its inspiration.

In December of 1932, Dorothy Day, former fre-
quenter of Communist and socialist circles, journalist, mother and recent Catholic convert, traveled
from her home on the Lower East Side of New York
City to Washington, D. C. in order to cover the
Hunger March of the Unemployed Councils and
the Farmers Convention. Both were led by com-
munists. Seven years later in her book, *House of
Hospitality*, Dorothy reflected on that march:

I watched that ragged horde and thought to
myself, "These are Christ's poor. He was a man
like other men, and He chose His friends
amongst the ordinary workers." These men feel
they have been betrayed by Christianity. Men

12

are not Christian today. If they were, this sight would not be possible. Far dearer in the sight of God perhaps are these hungry ragged ones, than all those smug, well-fed Christians who sit in their homes, cowering in fear of the communist menace.

As many Americans who lived through the first third of the twentieth century, Dorothy found herself caught in a dilemma. She understood capitalism to be a failure, a system that stripped the person of dignity and led to depression and to war. But the new messiah carrying the red banner of the social revolution, the voice of anger booming on the street corners of America, seemed to promise only violence and confrontation. Both systems affirmed only a material reality and thus a person's worth was defined either by how much capital he acquired, or how helpful he was in moving the historical process to a higher level. Neither capitalism nor communism could generate or sustain a spiritual vision. Dorothy continued to reflect on the unemployed and lamented her dilemma.

I felt that they were my people, that I was part of them. I had worked for them and with them in the past, and now I was a Catholic and could not be a communist. I could not join this united front of protest and I wanted to.

The next day, December 8th, the feast of the Immaculate Conception, Dorothy offered a prayer that a way would be shown for her to affirm the spiritual reality of God, and to work for the poor and the

13

oppressed. Her meeting with Peter Maurin was to show the way.

Peter Maurin was born in the Gevaudan area of Languedoc in the southern part of France to a peasant family in 1877. He was one of twenty-three children, all of whom grew up on the same land their ancestors had tilled continuously for fifteen hundred years. By the time he was twenty-eight, Peter had been a Christian Brother and had participated in a religious youth movement, LeSillon, which thought that the Catholic Church could speak to the modern social world. In 1909, he came to Canada as a homesteader. When his partner was killed in a hunting accident, Peter wandered around America taking odd jobs to support himself. Peter was an agitator, who became poor voluntarily, and when ca. 1933 he began his sojourns in New York City, he spoke in Union Square and stayed in flop houses on the Bowery. As a Catholic intellectual with a farming background, Peter envisioned a future where it would be easier for people to be good.

Peter read widely and his intellectual life had been influenced by diverse thinkers, social as well as religious. Peter Kropotkin and Jacques Maritain are but two thinkers who influenced Peter greatly. Never claiming to be an original thinker, Peter had an ability to synthesize seemingly diverse ideas into a whole. His synthesis was presented to the world in his *Easy Essays*, thought poems which outlined and argued for his new society. This society would combine an emphasis on the integrated person with a life shared in community and lived on the land. To a society characterized by industrial alienated labor, unemployment and poverty, Peter proposed a society built around the village, with people working the land, learning crafts, studying philosophy and science, participating in worship, and sharing life in common.

This was the society he wanted to move toward but Peter knew this vision had to grow, had to be nurtured among people who had lost sight of "simple truths" such as farming and crafts. So he developed a program of social reconstruction, a program which "would help us get from where we were to where we ought to be." This program had three parts: to develop houses of hospitality where the poor and the outcast could be fed, clothed, and sheltered, to encourage discussion groups that would help refine and further develop his vision of the good society, and to begin "agronomic universities" where people could learn farming and crafts and thus literally plant the seeds of the new society.

Peter, the traveling thinker, realized that he needed someone to help him put these ideas into concrete everyday living. He had read articles that Dorothy had written for Catholic magazines like *Sign* and *Commonweal*, and was determined that Dorothy should start on his program of social reconstruction. Peter arrived at Dorothy's house, which she shared with three friends and her child, the day before she returned from Washington. Her friends reminisced about the first time they met Peter.

He was wearing a khaki shirt and shabby stained pants and an overcoat, the pockets of which were crammed with books and papers.

15

When he started looking for something he pulled glasses out of his pocket (glasses that he bought for thirty cents and which magnified) and perched them half-way down his nose. For a year or so he wore a pair which had one earpiece missing so they sagged on one side of his face.

He began then, and continued for thirty years after Dorothy returned, to lecture on the poor, on justice, and on the need for a Catholic social reconstruction.

Peter resolved the dilemma that Dorothy had felt so poignantly while covering the Hunger March in Washington. He had drawn up a program of action which was simple and comprehensive. He felt it was not enough merely to bring the workers propaganda by way of a newspaper, pamphlets and leaflets. One must combine this with the direct action of the works of mercy: feeding the hungry, clothing the naked, sheltering the homeless, in order that one may instruct the ignorant, counsel the doubtful, and comfort the afflicted. The corporal and the spiritual works must go hand in hand, and getting out the *Catholic Worker* and distributing literature were, to Peter, performing spiritual works of mercy. For Dorothy the acts of feeding, clothing, and sheltering the poor recognized each person's special relationship with God in a way that capitalism and state communism could not. The act of making others aware of the possibilities of a new society through the *Catholic Worker* newspaper was a way of fulfilling her religious commitment in the social arena.

The begining of the Catholic Worker was not dramatic or rigorously planned. A French peasant wandering in Canada and America met a journalist who had recently converted to Catholicism. An intellectual with a vision sought out a person who was looking for a way of life and instruction. In her book *The Long Loneliness* (1952) Dorothy described the beginning of the Worker and its growth.

We were just sitting talking when Peter Maurin came in.

We were just sitting there talking when lines of people began to form, saying, "We need bread." We could not say, "Go, be thou filled." If there were six small loaves and a few fishes, we had to divide them. There was always bread.

We were just sitting there talking and people moved in on us. Let those who can take it, take it. Some moved out and that made room for more. And somehow the walls expanded.

It was as casual as all that, I often think. It just came about. It just happened . . .

It all happened while we sat there talking, and it is still going on.

Since the beginning in 1933, the Catholic Worker has lived out its beliefs with a fidelity which is peculiar to our age. Firmly believing in the autonomy and freedom of the person and the importance of one's ties to the land, the Worker has consistently supported decentralized forms of village and farm communities. Believing that one is personally responsible to the poor and the abandoned, Worker communities have typically been

17

established in the slum areas of our great cities. Convinced that one should return love for hate and violence, whether in the form of personal retaliation or state war, the Worker has consistently opposed all forms of violence.

For many who continue to struggle with the ethical and spiritual problems of our age, the Catholic Worker movement has become a symbol for good in the world. But the radical simplicity of Catholic Worker thought and way of life—the curious wedding of principle and action—remains a challenge to good intentions and a mystery to the scholar and sometimes to the Catholic Worker people themselves. It is this challenge which has called forth a growing literature that seeks, in essence, to define the Worker witness.

Writings about the Catholic Worker movement have generally fallen into two categories. The first group of writings have been written by people outside the movement, and are usually written about the movement or about certain personalities within the movement itself, such as Dorothy Day. In this general grouping the writers, typically, have visited Catholic Worker houses of hospitality for a week or two, and with this personal acquaintance, seek to tell the story of the Worker movement in terms of historical research and critical analysis. The best example of this approach is *A Harsh and Dreadful Love: Dorothy Day and the Catholic Worker Movement* (Garden City, New York: Image Books, 1974) by William D. Miller. This book while representing the best "distant-objective" analysis of Catholic Worker reality in terms of history, also provides some of the sharpest insights into the

heart of Worker life: its affirmations and perceptions of truth. *A Spectacle unto the World* (New
York: Viking Press, 1973) by Robert Coles and Jon
Erikson is another example of the literature *about*
the Catholic Worker, trying to combine a brief history of the movement, a short visit to the Worker
house in New York, and a pictorial portfolio.

The second group of writings have been written
by people inside the Catholic Worker movement.
The most prolific writer of this group is Dorothy
Day whose adult life has been lived within—and
thus has helped shape—Worker reality. Her literary attempts to explain and to clarify this reality are
to be found in her biographical reflections, *The
Long Loneliness* (New York: Harper and Row,
1952), *Loaves and Fishes* (Garden City, New York:
Harper and Row, 1963), her diary reflections,
House of Hospitality (New York: Sheed and Ward,
1939), and, combining both the biographical reference and day to day Worker life, in her monthly
column in the the *Catholic Worker* newspaper.
Much of the *Catholic Worker* newspaper
exemplifies this "inside the Worker" approach. The
reference point for most of this literature is not
scholarship or the historical story so much—
though this is written about—but the experience
of Worker life itself.

Both groupings, the "distant-objective" and the
"inside the Worker" approach, have the potential
for insight into the Worker movement. Both, of
course, have failings; the former tends to objectify
the personal and spiritual commitment of those
who have come to serve the poor and thus tends to
lose the day to day spiritual and physical sufferings

of the people at the Worker. A screen is thrown up; often we are not drawn in, or if we are, it is for someone else to serve and not us. The latter grouping has participated so much in Catholic Worker life that the experience can become a "closed-group" experience written in terms that are important to those who live and must work through these special trials, but when broached in the larger world fall on deaf ears, because of such different experience and language. Finally, there are limitations and restraints put on those daily involved with the same events and people. In order to keep relationships and happenings private and not public, and thus to preserve the trust of the people one is serving, personalities are rarely discussed, and a certain silence is both good and necessary.

This work attempts to take down the screen of the "distant-objective" analysis while refraining from a "closed-group" view of Catholic Worker life. My approach has differed from that of both literary genres because my experience in regard to the Catholic Worker was different. Instead of visiting for a few days, I lived at the Worker house and immersed myself completely into the life there for nine months (without any intentions of studying or writing for a public about my experience). After nine months, I left for graduate work at Florida State University. It was in this year of study that my experience at the Worker began to crystalize. It was also at this time that I began to realize the tremendous interest that my peers and my professors had for the day to day life as lived at the Worker house of hospitality. Many knew about the Workers' vision of a new society but the question I was most frequently asked was what it was like to live there. These diaries are an attempt to answer that question. As I responded to friends' queries about Catholic Worker life, I realized my perceptions made little sense without an understanding of where I was coming from when I arrived at the Worker in September 1974.

I was born and raised a Jew in the suburban city of North Miami Beach, Florida. When I say born and raised a Jew, I mean the secular Jewishness that has characterized so much of Jewish life in mid-twentieth century America. I attended Hebrew school until I was thirteen, had a Bar Mitzvah, and then quit Hebrew school altogether. I can remember asking the cantor, as I was practicing the prayers which I would chant in the synagogue, what the Hebrew words meant. Was I singing about Abraham, was I chanting the covenant after the Flood? He did not answer and I never knew.

I can remember also at that time being very concerned about the poor, and later when Bobby Kennedy was assassinated, I hung a poster of him on my bedroom wall.

College came. I immersed myself in a world of knowledge I had never known existed. It was stunning and exhilirating. At night I would prowl the corridors of the library pulling books off the shelves and reading them until the bell rang at midnight and the library closed.

As I moved on to my junior and senior years my concern for the oppressed reappeared. I had, by now, enough hours to complete my major in sociology and had embarked on a second major in religious studies. The study of institutions and the search for deep values sometimes confused me, but looking back it seems clear that a struggle for a vision that sought the changing of present social conditions as well as the affirmation of spiritual values, had begun. What this vision might be and where these social and spiritual values might come together I did not know.

My senior year was filled with indecision. What would my future bring? I applied to several graduate schools and was accepted at two, but I decided that this, at least for the time being, was not what I wanted. I felt an emptiness inside of me. Like many people on the college campus, I was filled with a thousand ideas about the nature of the human being, about the destructive aspects of our culture, and about the fragmenting quality of community. I saw what everyone else could see, that, in the midst of great affluence, there was poverty, in the midst of goodwill, war, and among the smiling crowd, a great and seemingly infinite loneliness. To me it seemed that I faced a dilemma similar to the one Dorothy Day faced in 1932. While I knew that there was something profoundly wrong in the way we were living, I could find no way to express this understanding in a constructive way. In my thirst for justice there was no love. I felt a great sense of being lost.

In the spring of 1974, a series of discussions were held on campus concerning the nature of the Catholic Worker movement. I had never heard of the Catholic Worker, but saw a leaflet describing the series and decided to attend. The discussions that followed seemed vague. Each Wednesday for six weeks, seven or eight of us gathered in the chapel of a local church and listened to tapes of Catholic Worker people speaking about their lives. Their stories were foreign to me. They talked about people who slept on sidewalks and people who were mentally deranged. Everyone was welcome regardless; craziness and violence were a part of life Worker people had learned to accept. It was hard to identify with these stories, what with living a suburban life most of my youth and then on a college campus. I remembered, though, that when I went to New York City to visit relatives, I was terrified at the sight of crippled veterans who held out tin cups and begged on the street corners.

After graduation I returned home to Miami, still undecided as to my future. I applied for several jobs, was interviewed twice, but found after a few weeks of job seeking that I really lacked the drive to secure a "regular" job. It was becoming increasingly clear that my ideas and views about life clashed with the jobs for which I was applying. I wanted to commit myself to work I believed in, but where was that type of work to be found?

As the month of August approached I began reading Dostoevsky's *Crime and Punishment*. The deeper I moved into the book the more I became convinced that the essence of the meeting of the major character, Raskolnikov, a murderer, and Sonia, a prostitute, was the search for commitment in the midst of suffering. Their meeting, like the meeting of Peter Maurin and Dorothy Day, provided the foundation for a life that was struggling to be reborn. Reflecting on my own life, I saw a similar need for guidance and rebirth.

Where this search might take me I did not know.

For the next two weeks I thought about it constantly and decided that I would go up to the Catholic Worker for a year. Though I had only a superficial understanding of what Catholic Worker life was like, I was fairly certain that the experience would be a challenge, perhaps even a struggle. I tried to prepare myself for a year that might raise more questions than provide answers. I was to learn that an encounter with suffering could not be prepared for by rigorous discipline or prior thought, and that a world turned upside down could transform a search into a trial by fire.

What follows is a journal of the year which I spent at the Catholic Worker on the Lower East Side of New York City. I want to emphasize that this is not the "definitive" statement about the Catholic Worker but *one* view of Worker life as it appeared to me (with my own concerns, peculiarities and shortcomings) during the year 1974-75. Others who shared the same experience might have seen things differently and would, perhaps, have stressed different themes. It is important to note also that the situation of Worker houses of hospitality often change quickly. For example in the past two years or so the amount of violence at the New York house has considerably lessened, and with the opening of Maryhouse, a new stability and strengthened community has developed. Any narrowness of vision is, of course, my own responsibility.

One hesitates to discuss personalities within the Worker movement. People in need have a right to their privacy: volunteers shy away from publicity.

Yet it is these people who are at the heart of the Worker movement, and thus inevitably become part of any writings of the Worker. Accordingly, I have changed names and drawn composite personalities at times. The diary entries have been edited for publication.

A work such as this could not have reached completion without a tremendous amount of encouragement and assistance. To my teachers at Florida State University, Ann M. Vater, Paul J. Piccard, Richard L. Rubenstein, Lawrence Cunningham, Charles Wellborn and William Rogers, I owe a special debt of gratitude. Through their example of study and concern they urged me to think and reflect. College was not an easy time for me and these teachers were often patient with my confusion. I am especially grateful for the presence and witness of William D. Miller, under whom I have studied at Florida State University and Marquette University. In allowing the freedom to think and write, Dr. Miller has been a steady guide, illuminating the main issues and possibilities of our time. To Lawrence Cunningham I extend my appreciation for helping me to prepare this manuscript for publication. The Department of History and the University Archives at Marquette University have been generous in assisting my continuing studies of the Catholic Worker movement. Thanks also to Robert Heyer, editor, who has been extremely patient and helpful.

Diary Reflections

September 4

Arrived at the East Side Terminal at one in the morning. I took a plane from Miami because to my surprise it cost less than a bus or a train. The airport farewell was typical. My mother and brother saw me off; my mother started to cry, then turned to my brother and said, "Marc is going to find his place in the world." I said goodbye to my father at home. Two years ago when I left for Europe my father cried. It was the first time I ever saw him cry and for a week afterward I had trouble falling asleep. I do not let him come to see me off anymore. It is hard for me to see my father cry.

Two blocks from the terminal I caught the Second Avenue bus which took me thirty-three blocks to East First Street. My bag was heavy, filled with fall and winter clothes. The bus took over an hour to come so I stood, bag at my side, on a semi-deserted sidewalk in the middle of the night. In the middle of Manhattan waiting for a bus! I was frightened at first; each approaching person evoked a certain fear. Finally the bus came and I boarded only to have an older woman lean across the aisle and start speaking to me. "Friend," she said, "awful dangerous to be carrying a big suitcase around like that in New York. Last week my son, who's a lot bigger than you are, was mugged carrying a suitcase just like yours." I winced as she continued, "Take my word for it." As the bus slowed to a stop I thanked the woman for her concern, and stepped into the night. What was my first impression? Desolation.

After walking in three different directions I finally found 36 East First Street. As I looked up at the building I saw that the balconies were decorated with purple streamers and orange confetti. Then I saw a sign: St. Joseph's House of Hospitality. The decorations were weird and it surely did not look like home. I had called the night before telling them when I would arrive. Each time a different person answered the phone so I was a bit uneasy about the assurance that a night watchman would be up and would let me in. I rang the doorbell, waited, and rang again but there was no answer. I saw a light in a second-floor window so I shouted hoping to catch someone there, but no one appeared. Can you imagine arriving in the Big Apple to find no one at home? Finally, a Puerto Rican man walking his dog asked me if I had come to work with "Miss Day." I said yes and told him that I could not get into the house. He directed me across the street where, as he put it, good people live. He climbed the steps, leaned across on a ledge, and rapped lightly on the window. He rapped two or three more times, each time a little louder, until a young man appeared in the doorway. He was slightly stooped, with eyes that seemed to reach out and to grab you. We shook hands, introduced ourselves—his name is Gene—and when I looked around the Puerto Rican man was gone. Gene led me into his apartment, rolled out a sleeper couch, brought a pillow and two blankets from another room, and said we would talk in the morning.

September 5

It is morning now and I am staring out the window. Across the street there is a long line of men waiting outside the Worker house. Above the men are the purple streamers and the orange confetti flapping in the wind, and a sign reading "The Catholic Worker, 36 East First Street."

Gene's apartment: two old chairs whose upholstery is badly worn; paint is chipping off the wall; the linoleum floor appears to be cracked all over; there is an old stereo (I wonder if it works); a light without a shade; and a few post cards hung on the wall for decoration. Very stark.

Across the street the line is growing. All men, some drinking, others pacing up and down. A few words and two men square off. Another steps in and the dispute is forgotten. Now a man is parading up and down the street cursing at the top of his voice, his head jerking back and forth. He is evidently in the midst of some kind of seizure. The pacing up and down, up and down, the cursing, and the heaviness of the buildings around him. A police officer sees the man and passes him by. The men on the line stand quietly outside. We all see this man becoming crazy. I feel a little dizzy.

The "good person" who put me up for the night is Gene Bellows. He invited me to have breakfast and afterward I used the sink for brushing my teeth. The kitchen, like the rest of the apartment, is bleak and contains, among the usual appliances, a bathtub which is on legs and in the corner. The washroom is a small cubicle.

It turns out that Gene is the editor of the *Catholic Worker*, an eight-page monthly newspaper the Worker supports. After breakfast, Gene took me across the street to the Worker house. The line was still growing and the men remained standing outside. We opened the door and, turning to our left, entered a room about fifty feet long and maybe twenty feet wide. Standing in the entrance I saw this: a desk on top of which a man was stretched out in a sleeping bag; ten or eleven chairs against the wall; two tables with twelve place settings on each table; a third table about six feet long on which vegetables were being cut by a young woman; an old cast iron stove and a separate lower burner behind her where a large pot of soup was being stirred. Contiguous with the dining area were a set of deep sinks. On the walls I saw a poster picturing a black man with the caption "Free Martin Sostre"; a Christ, his head with a crown of thorns cutting into his flesh; four post cards which I later learned covered up holes in the wall; a poster depicting Mahatma Gandhi; and finally a poster portrait of an American Indian with a poem for peace below.

Opening onto the street were three sets of windows—on the sill below a statue of St. Joseph—and through the back door I could see a bricked-in patio. With my eyes moving from the windows to the patio, I now saw four people eating breakfast, a person stirring the soup with a long wooden board, and three people, two of whom sat on metal boxes used to carry milk bottles, talking quietly on the patio. And then for the first time I saw a crucifix hanging on the red-bricked wall of the patio. At the base of the cross was a vase of beautifully arranged flowers.

Five minutes later people were busily at work. The patio emptied, breakfast ended and the table was cleared. The large pot which held the soup was lifted by a woman named Margaret and a black man introduced as Jack carried it toward the kitchen table and placed it on a wooden stool. Dishes were being washed, the tables reset, when finally—after a last minute check—the front door opened and the men who had waited outside rushed for seats at the table. It was nine-thirty in the morning.

As the men came into the Worker, Steve, a volunteer worker at the house, brought me up to the second floor and introduced me to a group of people sitting around tables, and then to Michael, the office manager, and John his assistant. Everyone seemed anxious to know where I was from and Ralph, an extremely large man with great sensitivity, began to talk to me about God.

Time passed, lunch and dinner were served, and then I was taken up to my room. The day itself was like a whirlwind, with new faces and a poverty I had never imagined in my life.

September 6

My room is a kitchen, and the space from the cabinets to the wall (the free space) is approximately four feet, three feet of which are taken up by the army cot. Length—thirteen feet divided in half by another mattress and my roommate, Robert, now lying on his floor bed. Since the kitchen facilities are no longer being used I have decided to store my books in the oven.

Our kitchen can be faithfully described as a semi-private room. My end of the kitchen opens out into the dormitory wing of the fifth floor but since Robert has a drape pulled across the entrance, our room though dark, and a bit musty (with most of his clothes hanging on nails around the room), retains a certain privacy.

Robert is drunk. It is now eleven o'clock and he has been reading newspapers, one after another, since seven o'clock; *The Boston Globe*, *The New York Post*, *The National Inquirer*, *Screw*. Though he is fifty-one years old, Robert informs me that he is still able to "get it up twice a week." To his question as to why I have come to the Worker I reply that I really do not know. Robert says that a guy my age "ought to be out getting laid. Geez, when I was your age, I was getting it everynight." Then he tells me a story about how once he had dates with two "dames" at the same time and place. I laughed. Finally, Robert says that he wants to show me all the hot places in New York, and that I am an "all-right kid not a religious nut like the rest of them."

But why have I come? Is it because I heard a group of lectures on the Worker last spring? Is it because I am lost? Will I find direction here? From Eliot good advice: "Teach us to care and not to care, Teach us to sit still."

September 7

Robert told me that I need to store my clothes down in Michael's office to prevent them from being stolen. This morning I went down to the second floor and asked Michael what I should do with my clothes. He advised me to put them in large garbage bags and place them in the corner of his office. I was apprehensive because there were piles of loose clothing already there, but Michael assured me it would be safe. With people dressed as lightly and casually as they were, I felt odd carrying around my suitcase full of clothes.

After I finished bagging my clothes I asked Michael what I could do to be of help. John, his assistant, suggested I go down to the first floor and work on the soup line. As I entered the first floor I was immediately struck by the smell of soiled clothes and cheap wine. These are the Bowery "bums" I have heard so much about I remember thinking. I found Steve and asked what I should do. The next two hours I spent washing dishes.

September 8

There is a community living here. The third floor is for women with two private rooms (one occupied by Dorothy) and five other beds in the big room occupied by women coming off the street and by female volunteer workers. Some of these women become permanent residents but most stay a few weeks or months and then leave. Two of the permanent women can hardly walk and leave their rooms only to come down to the first floor for lunch and dinner. They climb back up the stairs, slowly touching the steps ahead of them to maintain their balance and to gather the strength to continue climbing.

The fourth floor is for permanent male residents.

Mostly in their fifties, some of the men have been living at the Worker for ten years or more. As on the third floor, the large room is dormitory style with two semi-private rooms in the back. For a place as busy as the Worker, with well over five hundred people coming and going every day, these two floors remain fairly secluded, and for that reason, a bit mysterious.

The fifth floor is for transient men and male volunteer workers. I am in the kitchen with Robert, there are two private rooms on either end of the floor where permanent residents live, and the main floor is dormitory style. Some of the men here are down on their luck, or have mental problems; frequently both. All are unemployed and depressed. And why not? They have nothing that we would consider normal and healthy; a family who cares, a job that pays, or a place in society. In many ways they are cut off from the human family.

Being idle, people sleep at weird hours of the day. Don is a good example. He is about forty, cannot read and can only do "menial" jobs. He has no family and is unemployed. In the house, Don will mop the floors and the stairways, then he will come downstairs and wash dishes. But mostly Don will sleep, sometimes twenty hours a day. Every two weeks he will leave for two days and then return I am told. No one knows where he goes. His bed is saved and when he returns he is less and less coherent.

September 16

For the past three days—after the soupmeal—I have taken walks just to get away. The first day I

walked to the Metropolitan Museum of Art. Yesterday, I looked around used book stores. Robert
hooked up a light over my bed so I can read at night.
I started Dostoevsky's *The Idiot* but after reading
the first hundred pages I had to put it down. For
now, the written word has lost its meaning.

The fifth floor is gloomy with little light, brown-
gray walls, sagging beds, and lockers for clothes
instead of dressers. The bathroom is dirty and the
fear of bedbugs and lice is ever present. No privacy.
In the air a sense of doom.

The neighborhood is predominantly Puerto
Rican and one hears music blaring from private
clubs across the street till three or four in the morning. In the September warmth much of the social
activity goes on outside. It is noisy but good to know
that even this desolation affords some community.
Late at night you see women coming home well
dressed and in taxis.

September 19

The daily schedule. Nine to nine-thirty breakfast.
Usually about ten people show up. Volunteers and a
few people from the community. (The Quaker Oats
Company has just donated about six hundred
boxes of their natural cereal. Their "to be sold by"
date has passed, and until they are consumed they
will be our breakfast! With stale bread and concen-
trated milk.) Nine-thirty to eleven-fifteen, the
soupmeal. Anybody can come in for a bowl of hot
homemade soup, bread and tea. Most soupmeal
people come off the Bowery. They are homeless,
sick, often beat-up, sometimes crazy and/or violent, mostly walking in a stupor. Twenty men sit at

the tables, ten wait in seats against the wall, while forty sit in the basement on benches waiting for the first floor to empty. Often there are fights both at the table and in the basement. I have seen three knives drawn already. What does one do when a knife is drawn?

After the soupmeal, lunch is served from eleven-thirty to twelve-thirty. The community, comprised of the people who live and work in the house, and the Worker "family," those people who live in the neighborhood and have become friends of the community, are welcome. About fifty people attend lunch daily. Soup is served with bread, coffee, and tea. People from the "street" are barred until lunch is over thus encouraging a sense of participating in a shared meal with friends at "home." People sit in the same seats day after day and you are promptly informed if you have inadvertently sat in Ruth's or Larry's seat.

After lunch the tables are cleared, the floors swept, and the dinner menu decided. Between lunch (twelve-thirty) and dinner (five-thirty) the first floor is open to anyone who desires rest and community. Paradoxically, this is the time where violence occurs most frequently. By midday people who have no homes, drunks, junkies, the lost, often need outlets for their frustrations. Fights occur, windows are smashed; people are forcibly removed from the premises and others who resist too much are left to rant and rave, sometimes for hours. Certain individuals can, on any given day, completely terrorize the first floor and everybody there. But responsibility is not shifted to others; the police, as I understand it, are *never* called. Instead one tries,

37

in the midst of verbal and sometimes physical aggression, to carry on the day's activities (sweeping, washing dishes, pots and pans, helping people get clothes and shelter) as if everything were normal. A new normality.

Dinner is hectic. The community is served a sit-down meal by the volunteer workers. Meals are made from scratch so the dinner takes three hours or so to get together. The first table setting is for those who live in the house, the second setting for the "family," and the third setting for "street" people. Invariably persons from the first, second, and third settings overlap. Class and status lines sometimes develop. For example, some people who feel a part of the house dislike sitting near a "bum." This vast conglomeration of people at dinner leads to tension, and a fight or two (or three).

Tonight at dinner a man was being discouraged from coming around because of his continued violence. The plan was to keep him from eating until later when most of the community had left, but, having entered uninvited with the perpetual opening and closing of the front door, the plan was foiled and he was asked to leave. For him the Worker is home and when asked to come back later he turned and hit Steve, a volunteer, in the face. When Steve turned around the man was gone.

When dinner ends around seven, the dishes are cleared, the floor swept and mopped, and the place generally emptied. Some residents and friends go up to the second floor to watch television. At seven-thirty evening prayers are said on the first floor. Six or seven people attend. After Vespers, people gather to chat for a few minutes. The Worker remains open

till ten, and the time in between Vespers and closing is often quiet, and after the hectic pace of the
day, even peaceful.

But peace here seems the exception and the rule,
once spoken, is often broken. Last night during
Vespers, a man named Manuel came by, and being
drunk and told to sober up, forced his way into the
Worker. He would not listen to reason, refused to
leave or even to sit down quietly, and, instead,
paced up and down the floor cursing as he termed
them, the "saintly hypocrites." The prayers to my
amazement went on. It was alternately humorous,
sad, and beautiful.

September 20

I need more time to myself, some privacy. I have
begun to go aside in the morning and be still. This
gives me a chance to hear myself above the everyday
noise and activities. In the afternoon I have been
going to a library on Second Avenue and writing
some poetry trying to make sense of myself and the
Worker experience.

I came here looking for direction, for guidance
that would help me to sort out my understanding of
life. But there is very little support from the community. The people who work here come and go and
spend the major part of their life outside the
Worker. A new person is in a bad position; you have
no life outside the Worker and life inside is difficult.

Today I wrote about a building, old and crumbling, with stones becoming pebbles again and returning to the earth. At the doorway surrounded by
rubble, bruised and breathing the foul smell of
stones returning to the earth,

You crawl into a somewhat confused
And sometimes harrowing brightness
Symbol of passage, transition
Harbinger of new beginnings.

I hope.

September 21

My roommate Robert drinks a lot. Because of this excessive drinking our relationship has become strained. There are only two rules in the house: no violence and no drinking. Both rules are designed to encourage respect for "our" home. Since I saw Robert drinking and then witnessed his deteriorating condition, I asked people downstairs what I ought to do about it, if anything. The answer was a typical Worker response; we all take responsibility for each other. I was advised to make my position and that of the house clear. Telling Robert was difficult, partly because his hearing fails when he is admonished and partly because he is fifty and I am twenty-two. But tonight I was determined to make myself very clear; no drinking in the house! When I walked in Robert was lying on his mattress passed out. An hour later he tried to rise but could not. When he finally stood up he fell over. When he spoke, he made no sense. I became frightened. Jack told me not to expect Robert up for a few days, and when he did get up not to expect much coherence. Jack tells me that Robert has what Eugene O'Neil called the Brooklyn Boys, i.e., the D.T's.

Jack is an interesting man. He sleeps in the dormitory on the fifth floor right outside my room. He is black, probably about sixty and has lived here

40

for about a year. Policy here is that no one asks anyone about one's past life, but from conversation and observation I do know that Jack is sane, talented, and unemployed. (I also know that he plays a radio to help him fall asleep at night!) Jack cooks the soup two days a week, cooks dinner on Sundays, helps out in the morning when we are short-handed, and every so often watches the house at night. If Jack witnesses a fight or walks in on a heated argument, he walks by, and with a slight grin, shakes his head, spreads his hands palms up, and comments, "This is the way these guys are. I know that. And nothing's going to change them."

And Jack is right. People here have been through all the programs designed to help the alcoholic, the addict, the criminal, and those with mental problems. All are attempts to adjust the person to the society. Failures. I have learned that a number of people here, because they are poor and cannot afford proper medical care, have been treated by clinics and university medical schools where they were guinea pigs for new drugs and treatments.

September 22

All the activities of the Worker are carried on by voluntary labor. Essentially there are three types of volunteers: the permanent, the semi-permanent, and the transient.

Michael is an example of a permanent volunteer. Situated in the office, a small room in the back of the second floor, Michael could be called the business manager if the Worker were, in fact, a business. His duties: handle correspondence, record and dispense funds received (all through dona-

41

tion), keep expenditures within the budget, respond to requests by community members and family for monies, medical care, and any of a thousand other needs (light bulbs, brooms, cleanser, bus fare, etc.). Since Michael handles both the mail and the money, his office becomes the central focus of the community. His hours: eight in the morning to ten at night, six days a week.

Michael is in his fifties, of Boston-Irish descent, and a former executive with a large business firm in New York. As I understand it, Michael started coming to the Worker some years ago in his spare time. Later he quit his job and committed his life to the Worker house. By virtue of a strong faith, Michael works among the poor.

Gene can also be termed a permanent volunteer. Gene had been at the Worker for a few years when he refused induction into the military. As alternative service Gene chose to continue working at the Worker. Gene has strong convictions and became a conscientious objector because "the gospel preaches peace." He has already stayed beyond his required service and for the last two years has contributed to the Worker's spiritual and intellectual herald, the *Catholic Worker* newspaper. What the Worker preaches, Gene lives: voluntary poverty, performing the works of mercy at a personal sacrifice, combining the life of a worker and a scholar. At this moment Gene is the person most able to articulate the Worker's vision.

An example of a semi-permanent volunteer is Jim who plans to be here a year. Only twenty years old, Jim comes from a small farm town in Idaho and after a month and a half at the Worker is already adjusting to the Lower East Side. After high school, Jim entered the Franciscans but decided to take a year to explore his commitment further. This is not atypical of Worker volunteers. Jim is quiet, able to take on tremendous responsibility (much more and quicker than myself), and has a deep prayer life. He is both rugged and gentle, keeps to himself, and though he lives in the big room on the fifth floor, rarely fraternizes with anyone there including me.

Neal is a transient volunteer who will probably stay at the Worker for two or three weeks. And he sure brightens up the place! I am often advised by workers in the kitchen that "Neal does no work but when supper is ready he is always the first one downstairs." True, Neal does not do a lot of the basic tasks of Worker life, sweeping, washing dishes, etc., but he does do something of immense value: he meets people in the community personally, and being full of cheer he spreads joy throughout the house. While Jim is directed and determined that the structural aspects of the house function smoothly, Neal makes the structure meaningful in personal ways. These differences between Jim and Neal present a dichotomy in Worker life which is often a point of tension. If Jim removes someone for being boisterous then Neal's style is appreciated. And if dinner is late, Neal is the villain ("no good bum, free loader") and the call goes out for Jim to straighten the problem out. Neal will be here three weeks, Jim a year, and Michael may work here for twenty years, but all are needed for the Worker to exist, to function, and to be human.

September 25

I am writing this on the second floor. The soupmeal is over and I have decided to take a break. I have been here almost a month. Since I have arrived my contribution to the house has been washing dishes. Today I moved from the dishwater to serving soup at the tables. Basically I watch what is going on and try to make some sense of it all. The confusion in the morning is startling, and I just do not know how I would respond if I were in a more visible position, i.e., trying to direct the men to their seats, asking those who are violent to leave, and trying to bar Jody who has stabbed two people inside the Worker, one with a knife, another with a cooking fork, from coming inside. Frankly, I am still afraid.

Sitting across from me are two Sisters I have just recently met. Both are new at the Worker. Nancy is a Sister of the Sacred Heart, lives on Eighty-Second Street, and comes down to help three times a week. Ann is a Sister of St. Joseph from St. Louis and plans to live and work here for a year. Since we came to the Worker within a month of one another, we share the same bewilderment. We seem to be becoming friends.

People who work here, not as volunteers but because they have no home or job, add the explosive element to the internal Worker life and have an ability to disrupt the Worker community. I have been reminded of these working residents, because Louis has just thrown a metal garbage can against Michael's office door!! (Yesterday, he broke the backdoor window pane.) People are trying to calm him down but most people—and I am one of these—are trying to stay out of his way.

Louis is a man who has come unemployed, alone, and found a home here. He is a regular part of the house's work force. Most of the working residents, like Louis, are men in their fifties, unemployed, alone, often with physical ailments, sometimes mentally troubled, with a wide variety of life experiences, and rugged. Having little or nothing to fall back on, and fearing that the street awaits them, these workers often inject themselves into central positions within the community. For instance, Louis screens who is acceptable for residency in the house, while Ray, who helps out on the first floor, sometimes decides who is fit to eat in the Worker house. If the person is a "bum, a free loading son of a bitch," the possibility of residency for the night and food at dinner time diminishes. In these cases the permanent volunteers like Michael and Gene must insist that the Worker is open to all people. Semi-permanent volunteers are caught in the middle, unable to command enough authority to do what is right, and open to the wrath of the working residents.

Obviously there are a number of factors entering into this tension, the first derived from the working resident's lack of place in society, and the second an increased resentment to middle class "punks" trying to run things their own way. I can understand this tension but what is important here is the possibility of a few strong individuals tending to dominate the community. Admittedly it is not all bad. Louis is often nice to me, and Ray an ex-seaman who confesses to liking me has only threatened me with death twice.

September 26

The men I wrote about yesterday in terms of their struggle for positions of power may, in fact, be the exceptions to the rule. Unfortunately, the exceptions often determine the atmosphere of the house. Perhaps the working residents are more like the man who has just emerged from Michael's office, tapped me on the shoulder, and when I told him, in jest, that I was engaged in serious writing, took a step back and exclaimed in a high pitched voice, "Don't pick on me." And in his usual style he continues by appealing to others around the room, lifting his hands as if in need of rescue and saying, "He's picking on me. Tell him to stop picking on me."

The man's name is John. He is fifty-one years old, five foot six, one hundred and ten pounds, sender of the mail, recorder of the contributions in the ledger book, and bringer of the newspaper copy to the press. John and I are becoming good friends usually spending time together when he ventures forth from his private room on the fifth floor to the dormitory room. He appears in his long white nightgown, tells me to retire to my "room," tells the others to quiet down and go to sleep, and then promptly sits down and begins to talk.

John was orphaned at a young age and lived in institutions most of his childhood. It appears that John became somewhat of a hobo, traveling quite a bit, going to homes to beg lodging and food for the night, taking odd jobs for a few weeks or so, and then moving on. Though I am unclear how John found the Worker, I do know that he has lived and worked here for over twenty years. John is extremely religious, attending Mass daily, and on Friday nights going to services at the Salvation Army where, as he puts it, "my friends are." Being so religious and so meek, and constantly asking people he knows for money, John is affectionately known as the Bishop of the Bowery. Holding out a small change purse, looking as deprived as possible, John solicits contributions for the "Bishop's Relief Fund."

Across the table Ruth is laughing. It is nice to hear her laugh. Her life, in many ways, is tragic, but God has blessed her with an inability to perceive her burden. Ruth is retarded. Her children have been taken away from her, and she goes with men whom she introduces as her "husband." The nights she does not go out, she sleeps on a bench in the basement. Her clothes are rarely washed; she is unaware of her bodily functions and her obesity adds to her problem of cleanliness. Ruth is often covered with dirt, speaks a language that is hard to decipher, but after hearing her say hello every morning and watching her smile, one doesn't hesitate to give her a big hug. Ruth loves to "read" books and right now she is in the midst of the autobiography of Goethe, insisting that the book is a detective story filled with "a lot of murders." Ruth loves to knit, but when supplies are scarce, like today, Ruth knits with kite string. She can get angry, though, especially when one of her sleeping companions in the basement is thought to have stolen her clothes. Usually however, Ruth is peaceful and praises God. Here amidst this suffering—a glimpse of grace.

Two other men are at the table, one sleeping (he was walking around the streets all night because he had no money for a "flop") and the other so drunk that he has passed out. Two weary heads resting on the table, Ruth knitting in the corner, and a framed picture of the Virgin Mary hanging on the wall; meditations on poverty and on the spirit.

There are other women at the Worker. Edna, a frail black woman, crouches in the corner and speaks rapidly to a person deeply imbedded in her imagination, advising him to leave her alone, to "get away from me." Two or three times a month she reappears after a day's absence with bandages wrapped around her head and face. At other times she will launch into a deep, cultured voice and parade boldly around the room as if in a play. Edna is one of Ruth's roommates in the basement.

Women who come to the soupmeal are more easily accepted into the Worker family than the men so a number of soupmeal women are present at lunch and dinner. Still three or four women show up every morning. Yesterday a woman came in whom I have seen here before. She is Southern with beautiful features, but with a mind that has snapped. She gestures rapidly, salutes people who serve her, stares off into the distance, talks wildly, then covers her eyes with a stiff hand, looks at her soup and begins to eat. Her hands shake so that she must lift the bowl to her lips to drink the soup. What has brought her here? Where does she live? Does she live with the woman I talked to yesterday, sporting a crewcut and being nine months pregnant, malnourished, homeless, and still refusing a bed at the Worker? If so, she lives in a doorway.

September 27

I checked Perkins into a Bowery "hotel" tonight. This is a regular practice of the Worker. If there are no more beds left at the house for the night, we accompany the man to the hotel and pay his fare. The price is two dollars and twenty-five cents for the night. We accompany him for two reasons: to provide a sense of community and to insure that the money is not spent for drink. These "hotels" are really flophouses filled with violence and bedbugs. The city refuses either to establish or enforce minimum safety and health standards.

Perkins is a regular member of our newspaper operation, an operation which consists of folding, labeling, and sending out eighty thousand *Catholic Worker* newspapers nine times a year. For twenty days a month he and about twelve other unpaid members of the family are busy at work on the second floor. But Perkins is also an alcoholic. Once a month he starts to drink until he is so stooped over he can hardly stand. And he simply does not care to live at the Worker house. So even though Perkins has worked faithfully at the Worker for a number of years, and earns more than his keep, he prefers the Bowery flops.

October 1

Every Tuesday from one to five in the afternoon, the clothing room, which is an abandoned building across the street that we rent from the city for one dollar a month, is opened to serve men in need of clothing. (Wednesday is for women.) Steve is the person who stocks the donated articles during the week and gives the articles away on Tuesday. While I was eating soup today I inquired about how the clothing distribution worked so he suggested that I help him after lunch.

The room used is about twenty feet wide and perhaps seventy feet long. Inside are boxes filled with specific types of clothing from underwear to winter coats, all to be given away free. The men line up outside and one man is allowed in at a time. For many men this is the time when they change the clothing they have been wearing for the week. Their old clothes are thrown out.

Even this service has its share of violence. Last week Steve was beaten up pretty badly. Why? Steve will not talk about it. From others in the community I heard that much of what is given away here is sold by the men to used clothes dealers for money to drink. After the last man left I asked Steve if what I had heard was true, and, if it were true, what that meant to him and to the idea of the clothing room. He said that if only one person in a hundred needed these clothes, it was worth the effort, and that a Christian was not oriented toward success per se but toward service. And then as quickly as he began to speak he became silent.

Afterward I walked over to Washington Square Park across from New York University. I thought about going into their library but three police officers guarded the entrance. A few minutes later I found myself sitting in a chapel reflecting on the postscript of Dorothy's autobiography, *The Long Loneliness*:

The most significant thing about the Catholic Worker is poverty, some say.

The most significant thing is community, others say. We are not alone anymore.

But the final word is love. At times it has been, in the words of Father Zossima, a harsh and dreadful thing, and our very faith has been tried through fire.

And then I thought of Steve.

October 7

I have seen Dorothy several times and have spoken with her twice. At least since I have been here, she has been living in a small cabin on Staten Island and comes to the Worker for a few days at a time. Dorothy is seventy-six years old, and has long gray hair usually put up and covered with a scarf. Her face is highlighted by high cheekbones and a carved thinness. She is beautiful.

I really did not know what it would be like to meet her. Would she have time to speak to others or were so many people trying to meet her that to preserve her strength and sanity, she would say hello and move on? I found the contrary to be true. Dorothy is warm, wanting to know about you and your background, and often relates stories of her own life to you. She loves company. Today, for instance, a visitor came to see her and as I walked by she invited me to stay for tea. The discussion started with Father Dan Berrigan, a radical Jesuit priest, and ended with stories about her good friend Eugene O'Neil, the famous American dramatist. She told how O'Neil's tragedies were inspired by great love. To Dorothy his plays were confessions, a searching for a forgiveness that he never found.

Dorothy loves to travel, and her day to day influence on the affairs of the house is small. She is, as she remarks with a smile, retired, but the important decisions are still referred to her.

My talks with Dorothy have revealed several recurring themes of hers. She draws a distinction between a poverty freely chosen in community and a forced destitution without community. The freely chosen poverty in community is, for Dorothy, a response to the Gospel message which calls for a non-attachment to material goods as well as a shared spiritual life. Forced destitution, on the other hand, represents the evils of our present society which does not care for others, and reduces people to economic, social and spiritual obscurity. Dorothy refuses to see herself as an intellectual but instead as a disciple. She consistently speaks of Peter Maurin as the founder of the Worker and as her teacher. Her role is to embody his principles and present them to the world. Dorothy places a heavy emphasis on the need for repentance and confession. "If only we would recognize our sins, confess them to others and truly ask forgiveness," she often says, "our hearts would be changed and grave injustices would be overturned." Finally, Dorothy insists that people are called to a vocation and that each person's calling is different. (To me she said that I should not feel guilty if I found my vocation outside the Worker.)

Dorothy scoffs at herself being considered a saint by others. Though she is sweet with smiles, and affectionate with the community and visitors, the Worker was built and has survived not on these qualities alone but because Dorothy was and is both tough and inspirational.

October 8

The Bowery is an intrinsic part of Worker life. Ninety per cent of the soup and clothing distribution goes to Bowery people. The street itself, located three blocks from the Worker, is desolate: a major throughway with warehouses, flophouses, and bars.

Walking a person to a "hotel" at night provides this scenery: perhaps a hundred men walking in groups of two or three on the sidewalk, many times with whiskey flasks in their hands; three or four all male bars, and ten or fifteen men in rags waiting at the lights for cars to stop, then "cleaning" the windshield of the stopped car and asking for a donation in return. Many of the men are so drunk that they meander through oncoming traffic. The median invariably contains one or two men who have passed out or writhe in convulsions.

I wonder if I can convey the picture of this street at all. Abandoned by the political community in terms of services (garbage collection, police protection, etc.), abandoned by the social community (no permanent residents, no enforcement of laws against public drunkenness, or obscenity—one can see two men copulating or one masturbating on the street corner), a whole population of wandering half-men drowning in a sea of dark brick, semi-trucks, and disease.

October 9

I walked by the municipal shelter last night on East Third Street which is a big hall for the homeless to eat during the day and to sleep at night. Before the shelter opened for the night I saw a hundred men lying on the sidewalk.

October 12

My roommate Robert has been warned about his drinking, and has a great fear that he is being forced out of the house. Eight months ago Robert was found wandering around the garment district broke and hungry. He had had an accident which impaired his hearing and his equilibrium. It should be better now, but Robert has no intention of leaving. He has no place to go and no one to go to. Anyway, Robert is on everyone's nerves; he refuses to let anyone near "his" kitchen, accuses people out in the big room of stealing his stuff (which he picks off park benches and out of garbage cans) and has now refused to speak to me, saying only that I am a traitor, a young punk who was all right and now has turned against him. When there is an empty bed in the big room I intend to move out there.

October 14

What is happening here? After a month and a half at the Worker I can honestly make a few statements: the Worker feeds people who are hungry, clothes people who are naked, and shelters people who are homeless. The Worker serves those who are abandoned, survives on donations and free labor, and has a community living under its roof.

I am at the mercy of the people here who alternately praise me for a heart of love which I doubt I have, and chastise me for things I have no control over: my youth, family, education, and hope. They keep me honest if a bit confused. Ralph is one of those people. Each morning I am a revelation to him. Either I have crossed him and am a devil or I have awakened a truth in him and am a saint. Joan, especially, will tell me at any moment of the day that I have no right to be here, that I know nothing of life, and that I must get some kind of kick looking and visiting with the poor. Joan, a former successful artist, sleeps on a bench in our basement. She is right. I have no idea of what it is like to be poor or to be totally broken. There are no pretensions here.

October 18

Walter Cronkite. People who live here and "family" outsiders gather around the tables; those who cannot find seats stand in the rear of the room. The room is cluttered with eighty thousand *Worker* newspapers. A third of the papers have been folded, and the labeling of that third is, for a few stalwarts, continuing into the night. But for most of the newspaper crew, volunteers and guests, the day is drawing to a close. How nice to see a man with coat and tie (and a set of teeth) telling us in words and pictures what the state of the world is "really" like. A few of the news items: Jewish mothers in Brooklyn face a group of angry blacks who demand that public housing be allowed in this upper middle-class residential area, tax cut imminent, welfare rolls being cut back. The room is filled with people who have no homes, no income, and most without welfare, yet the reaction to Cronkite's reporting betrays an identification with the powers that be. The people gathered agree that the Jewish mothers have worked hard and deserve a neighborhood free of public housing, all agree that taxes need to be cut and that the welfare rolls need to be cleansed. "What kind of country is this turning into anyway?" Walter provides an "in" to a community which denies their existence. Reflections on images and tyranny.

October 26

How can one convey to another the poverty here? The simple facts of life for the Bowery person and the poor of the Lower East Side? That there is no privacy, that clothes worn are donated, that bathrooms are shared by many people, that one can never eat alone, and instead is continually forced to live a communal life? Should I say that most are not "bums" but abandoned poor: the unemployed, the elderly, the retarded, the addict? That these people have not chosen their abandonment but have been created by a society and then cast off into this darkness?

Coherence. Can this diary be coherent? Can there be a progression where there is, by example, no progress? Can one organize the situation, structure this life, in a sense help it to assume a certain hope where now there is only hopelessness?

Here life is not a chapter by chapter proposition where an intricate plot can be woven into a neat solution. Here there are only a hundred faces by day, a fight, an insult, a thousand nights of being beholden, scared, and abandoned. Here the only deliverance is death. And it is much more difficult to die here than one might expect.

October 31

Before coming to the Worker I had never seen people who, having lost their original teeth, had not replaced them with dentures. Nor did I know anyone who did not change clothes and shower every day. Tonight, sitting against the wall waiting to eat supper, I counted twenty people at the table, twelve of whom had no teeth.

November 5

Further reflections. My arrival in September was not met with any kind of enthusiasm and the first few days of my stay here were, to say the least, confusing. The people here were quite a change from the "regular" people I was accustomed to, and the discussions I came to have with Worker people left me unable to distinguish between fact and fantasy. People assumed masks and believed in their new identities. Rachel, dressed in three layers of used army coats (with medals), a large uncombed wig, and a heavily made-up face, insisted that she was a teacher on special assignment. Annette took the role of a religious, a nun who came to save souls tending toward hell. Fantasy became fact; reality was no longer real. For a week I began to question my own "facts."

At first my work consisted solely of doing dishes and, in the slack periods, looking up to see the happenings at the soupmeal. I was appalled by the violence, by the looks and the sickness of the men, and by their drunkenness. I had suddenly been tossed into a world of brutality and evil where all meaning had collapsed.

As the days passed, I found that the community of workers and scholars that I was prepared by the lectures to expect, did not exist, that there was, in actual fact, little community at all. There were no meetings designed to help clarify thought.

The first month, then, was consumed in an attempt to deal with total reversals: the strange types of people, the absence of community, of intellectual focus, and above all, the lack of support and welcome. A person coming here was simply left alone to drift (usually sink) in an alien environment. Finally, the volunteers seemed to be almost as odd as the people who filled the first floor from morning to night. They were so quiet, so withdrawn and somber, that I appeared to be a loudmouth, a jester. I could perceive absolutely no joy here at all. Perhaps it was because they were so tired.

These first impressions have gradually given way to more authentic perceptions but there remains some truth in these first observations. The Worker is not a typical place and I doubt that there are any adequate preparations for a journey here.

November 9

If you come here without any illusions, which I prided myself on doing, you are still prone to psychic kicks in the groin. Today is the third day of severe stomach cramps for me. I hope it is not an ulcer.

November 10

My roommate, Robert, has decided that a trip to the bathroom is too tiring what with his drinking and his weak bladder. Instead he urinates while lying in bed, in a jar which he leaves standing in the middle of our room until it is full. After he urinates, he conscientiously screws the top back on the jar, emits a sigh of relief, puffs up his pillow and begins to read another newspaper. I pretend not to notice but it is not easy.

November 12

Tomorrow I am scheduled to "take the house." From breakfast until lunch the people working the soupmeal and serving lunch are co-responsible for the safety of the house, i.e., halting confrontations which are leading to verbal and physical violence, and the barring of those who are drunk or drugged, handling requests for food, shelter and clothing, and keeping the first floor and the dishes clean. When lunch begins, one person becomes responsible for all those duties until dinner, when another person assumes responsibility until ten at night. When the burden shifts to one person that person is said to be "taking the house." In essence, the person taking the house is solely responsible for serving those in need and keeping some sense of order and peace.

I have witnessed afternoons when one of the community's friends, drunk and hostile, will keep the Worker, and thus the person taking the house as well, under siege all day long. When the volunteer steps outside to ask the man to cease breaking the front windows, he responds by swinging a two by four piece of lumber by her head. Taking the house means, among many things, a willingness to accept violence without retaliation. It also means the beginning of a battle to win the respect of the house you are called on to watch over.

November 13

Thank God it is over! When Jim came to take the dinner shift, all I could do was to come upstairs and fall asleep. Actually, very little went on today, just the routine of sweeping, doing dishes, and answering the phone and the door. But you get tired just knowing that at any second violence can spring up; from a little joke, a bit too much to drink, or simply from nowhere and for no reason.

Some goings on today. The cook yelled at me for letting a Bowery person (a "bum, who shit in his pants") in for leftover soup. He had not eaten in two days. Received a call from a woman in her ninth month of pregnancy. Abandoned by the father, welfare has given her a place to stay and foodstamps, but no furniture. She has been sleeping on the floor for a week. She asked if we might have an extra bed. A man called on the phone asking if we would be interested in a donation of thermal underclothing. When I asked how much he had to donate he said, matter of factly, five thousand pairs. Two welfare workers called up trying to find lodging for homeless people. Should I have suggested opening their own homes to the homeless?

Have just been advised that Ray took Jim by the collar and threatened to hit him if he let one more "bum" in during dinner. Yesterday Henry, who also works in the kitchen and has been at the Worker for over ten years, threw scalding soup on another volunteer. The tensions between the volunteers and the working residents are increasing. A meeting has been set for two weeks from tonight. Maybe I will get to know the volunteers better.

November 14

Bruce is what most people would call a bum. And a violent one at that. He has frequented the Bowery for several years and often comes by the Worker. Bruce looks to be about forty. His hair is stringy and thinning on top, and he has lost his original teeth. The first time I saw Bruce he was drunk, trying to get by Steve at the door, cursing and kicking him in the shins. Four hours later he was sobered up, apologizing to Steve and conversing with others as if they were long lost friends. I marveled at the change of behavior and wondered what shape Bruce would be in when I encountered him at the door.

Will is another "bum" I wonder about. Will is extremely well educated and used to teach in an exclusive prep school in Maine. He married into wealth and even now receives checks each month from his wife. His money does not last long on the Bowery. He uses it either to buy drinks for himself and his companions or he is rolled in an alleyway. When Will is drunk he becomes obnoxious and often violent. Sober, he is friendly and intelligent.

This morning the temperature was thirty-seven degrees. The cold has begun. The line for soup outside the Worker grows steadily. We try to let the men in earlier each morning and allow them to sit in the basement. Despite the cold weather this morning, I spotted four men in the line in short sleeves. Some sold their coats for liquor, others had their coats stolen during the night. I went upstairs and found four coats.

November 15

During the fall and spring, Friday night meetings are held on the first floor. This is in keeping with the round table discussions Peter Maurin felt were so essential in working out the principles and the details of the new society. A speaker is invited and the topic of his/her talk is publicized in the Worker newspaper. People come from all over New York City. With the benches up from the basement and the tables taken down, forty people can be accomodated. The topics range from communitarian lifestyles to the discussion of non-violent strategies for the future.

Tonight Henry Nouwen was our speaker. He is a well known Catholic writer and is concerned with such topics as healing and ministries for the dispossessed. His topic was "Christianity and the Christ Room." Each home, he said, should have a room for the wanderer, and those without shelter. It is a space set aside for caring and healing, a room, in essence, for others. The term "Christ room" denotes the welcoming of a stranger as one would welcome the Messiah.

The talk was a good one. Nouwen emphasized the connection between caring for another and the ability to cure. Without care, he said, there could be no cure of mental illness, feelings of abandonment, or criminal behavior. His words described a reality that I experience every day. Programs for every conceivable malady are available, and many here have been through these programs. But the fact of people's lives here is that no one has cared enough for them to make the cure they have received remain.

November 19

Dave is seventeen. His parents are dead, and his home consists of the Worker, people who will take him in, and the street. Dave is retarded, epileptic, and a former addict, so his fourth home is, as he terms it, the psycho ward at Bellevue Hospital. Today, Dave went into convulsions. Jim and I wrestled him down, hailed a cab, and took him into the walk-in clinic at Bellevue. I agreed to wait with Dave.

It is hard to describe the walk-in clinic at Bellevue. Some call it a trash can, for the poor, the criminal, the "bum" are all thrown here. There seem to be more guards than doctors and nurses. I remember several scenes so vividly that they become present again. An eighty-four year old man who wanders around the city by day and sleeps in the gutter at night, bloodied by a blow to the head, delirious, clothed as if it were a summer day, is asked if he has any children. He cannot remember. A poor Puerto Rican family has been waiting two hours to have their child's bandaged hand looked at by a doctor. Already possessing a hard street appearance, a young man doubles over in the corner. An orderly finally gets him care. Two police officers bring in for a physical examination a man who has just been arrested. His hands are manacled behind his back.

For the number of people, the suffering, and the long delays, one would expect a host of complaints.

But the poor are used both to the filth and to their station in life. One even wonders if they aren't thankful: they certainly make few demands.

November 27

After working the soupmeal this morning I went to Bellevue to visit Dave who was recommitted to the mental ward yesterday. After ringing the buzzer and being checked over, I entered the ward's lobby. It was like entering a strange world. I saw three people who frequent the Worker walking the halls. Music was blaring and when Dave appeared I noticed that he had been heavily drugged. During our conversation, many people walked by—all under seemingly heavy medication. Is this therapy? Meeting of the volunteers tonight at seven-thirty.

The meeting was a success. Finally I learned a little more about the volunteers. Jeff's apartment was used instead of Gene's. Jeff's apartment is across and down the street from the Worker. We arrived on the fifth floor after climbing a steep, winding, and poorly lit staircase. The building is a slum; dark corridors, five or six people to a room, the constant fear of violence. Mostly Puerto Rican tenants. When six people were present we all sat down and, well, remained silent. Incredibly silent people. With a sort of anxious curiosity I began with a question, "Could we introduce ourselves to each other? I've been here almost three months and I hardly know anyone." This is what I found out.

Sharon is twenty-eight years old, grew up in Boston, and describes herself as a ghetto Catholic; Irish, poor, (she was raised in public housing). After graduating from college, she worked as a

64

teacher, but sensing an emptiness and having read the Worker newspaper since fourteen, she came to find out what the Worker was all about. That was three years ago. Sharon has a good sense of humor, is fearless—I have seen her slugged and spat upon without budging an inch from her considered truth—and lives a life of poverty. Her apartment, right across the street from Jeff's, is sparse, and dark. Sharon rents the apartment alone but rarely is without guests, i.e., people in need. For the last three weeks a three member family has been staying with her in the "other" room. All her clothes come from donations; she is employed for money on a part-time basis in order to pay her rent. Sharon remains single, living and working among the poor, and waiting on God.

Jeff is nineteen, an unbelievably young age to be at the Worker. Because Jeff is so very quiet I know little about him. He is medium height, thin, with straight brown hair, and usually wears an old pair of Converse sneakers. Jeff came here straight out of high school two years ago. Miscellaneous: his parents live in Ohio, he takes long trips sometimes disappearing for weeks, he rarely smiles, and is extremely tough. Jeff is insightful and is the only person who can communicate with Ray. Young, intense, and interesting.

Margaret is twenty-six years old, tall, with long brown hair that is usually swept back and covered with a scarf. Born in New York City of a low-income, working-class family she, like Sharon, describes herself as a believer since birth and attends Mass daily. Margaret is quiet and determined but always ready for a joke. She has a masters degree and, though she taught exceptional children for two

65

years, prefers to devote her full energies to the Worker house. She does substitute teaching to earn her rent money. She hustles men out of the Worker with ease and takes little nonsense. A person of insight, Margaret reads for the Spirit and lives it.

Steve: twenty-six years old, short, sturdy build, glasses, balding. He has an aura of meditation about him and reads, among others, Dostoevsky, Kafka, and Simone Weil. Steve was brought up in Europe, and returned to America to graduate from New York University with a major in Government. After graduation he refused induction into the army, went to Canada for two years, and then returned and served in the army for two years as a medical orderly. Steve describes college as a confused time and his decision to enter the army even as an orderly as something, "I'm not sure was right." He is so forgiving that two days ago when I stepped between him and another man who was hitting Steve in the face, and then told the man that he should not come around for a few days, Steve tapped me on the shoulder and told me I should not be so harsh, that the man was tired and hungry and hardly to blame. An hour later the man returned, his legs and feet bloodied. I was standing in the doorway enjoying a rare quiet hour at the Worker, and as I looked in, I could see Steve listening to the man's laments, and quietly, as if in a state of prayer, washing the man's feet.

November 28

I was awakened early this morning by John who told me that I was needed downstairs right away. I threw on a pair of pants and raced downstairs. By the time I arrived the emergency had ended. Two tables filled with cups and bowls for breakfast had been overturned and Alex, a robust Spanish man with curly hair, his bathrobe hanging open and his head jerking back and forth in rhythmic spasms, was pacing up and down the room. As he paced, he pointed his finger at Margaret repeatedly telling her to "get screwed you damn whore. Do you hear me? No one's going to cage me in, whore!" During the outburst Margaret continued to stir the soup and after Alex had calmed down she pulled a chair up to his desk and began talking with him.

Alex is in his forties, lives a great part of his life, except for occasional walks, within an area of ten square feet. At the very front of the fourth floor is Alex's home, a chair where he sits during the day, and a table on top of which he sleeps during the night. About once a week he explodes but never touches a soul. What is wrong with him? Where does he come from? All we know is that he is part of the family, which brings me back to the central focus of the meeting last night: the Gospels. Gene said that "insofar as we adhere to the Gospel we are approaching truth. That is the Worker's measuring rod. The works of mercy at a personal sacrifice. Community for all of creation." No turning your back on violence and sickness here, or hiring people to take care of it for you. Forgiveness at the Worker is no platitude, no ideal, but a reality. St. John of the Cross said, "And where there is no love, put love, and you shall find love."

November 29

No easy way to describe the tension. Tonight two regular visitors were asked to leave for extended verbal clashes. They asked Steve to step outside to talk the problem over, and when he obliged, a flurry of punches hit him square in the face. Steve refused to fight back or even to protect himself. Nothing deters these people, even the intervention of five or six people. Equally interesting is Steve's ability to explain the violence by recounting life histories and the daily experiences of the assailants. Dave — who was one of the assailants — had just given two pints of blood in order to get enough money to go drinking. Steve said this made Dave tired and irritable.

Are the grotesque, the outcast, the violent, caused by the city, New York? Do they inevitably result from a social milieu that does not emphasize, but even helps to defeat, attempts at community?

December 5

Today I sat in the basement with the men waiting for soup. The walls are lined with benches, and I am there to make sure that the men sit down in the order they come in and, when the first floor empties, go up single file in the order that they should. The men are usually cooperative; any trouble that does erupt must be quelled quickly.

Looking around this morning I could see that these Bowery "bums" could not be stereotyped. The men are young and old and middle-aged, black and white and brown, Jewish, Protestant, and Catholic, immigrant and third or fourth generation American. They are mostly somber; faces with no expression. Their ailments vary; many have tuberculosis and sores all over their bodies, few have teeth, most are lousy. The men become oblivious to the world, and walk through life like dead men. There is no pretense of hope among them; history and the future are categories that are dealt with only in yesterday and tomorrow. The eternal present is left; a harsh eternity. But is it not true that among these bent bodies and bowed heads, perhaps in the corner patiently waiting to be served a bowl of soup, is Jesus himself?

This, it seems, is the pivotal point of Catholic Worker life. If, in fact, Jesus could or would not appear here in the basement, if his words, "I say to you, as long as you did it to one of these my least brethern, you did it to me," (Mt. 25:40) were not incarnated truth, then the Worker position would slip from the realm of truth to the realm of good works and finally to absurdity. The Worker is totally radical; it believes in an all encompassing spiritual reality here on earth.

December 9

Sacred space. Tonight (and every Monday night) Mass is said at the Worker. Father Lyle, who runs a half-way house in Harlem presides and other religious in the Worker family enter the house for fellowship and community. Among these people are the Little Brothers of Jesus who live and work among the poor, and ex-Worker volunteers like Pierre who is in the process of extraditing three autistic persons from the state mental hospital promising that he will be a parent to them for life. When you add to the company the Worker household, and the fact that the service is held on the first floor where destitution, insanity, and violence fill the very walls, then it is hard to describe the overwhelming sense of love that transforms this madness into the sacred. Without embellishment, and

69

only with the Word and a people, a scratched and battered table which bears soup for the dispossessed in the morning bears by night the blood of the Lamb "who takes away the sins of the world." And for a strange moment the soup and the blood, the dispossessed and the Messiah, Jesus, become one.

December 10

Last night at about ten o'clock the buzzer rang. Mass had been over for an hour and the first floor was almost empty. I was in the back finishing off the last of the dishes and by the time I opened the door there was no one outside. As I closed the door I turned and saw Leslie, a woman I know from the soupmeal, naked from the waist up. I averted my eyes and I heard her say that she was sorry. She was in the midst of changing her clothes and I told her to go into the bathroom to finish.

Leslie is in her middle forties and often wraps sweaters and shirts around her legs instead of wearing skirts or pants. Her face, especially, is almost always visibly dirty and I have to tell her constantly to button her shirt or rearrange her clothing so she is not exposed. A few minutes later I knocked on the bathroom door and told her I was closing for the night. She came out of the bathroom and took her two bags, said, "Thank you," and stepped outside. She has no home. I wonder where she sleeps.

During the last week or so I have had to tell ten people that we have no beds available. Sometimes the person just shrugs her shoulders and looks for another place. They are used to being sent on their way. Others plead for any type of shelter. They know of nowhere else to look. Every night people, like Leslie, leave the Worker with nowhere to go. It is one thing to speculate as you are walking down the street where and how a down and out looking person eats and sleeps. The street allows a certain distance. It is another thing to know the people themselves and their situation, or to be asked personally for assistance. Two nights ago a mother and her two young boys came by in the evening for a place to stay. They had been sent by Catholic Charities. We had no place to put them and no place to recommend. I told the mother that they were welcome to eat here three times a day and that I was sorry.

December 13

Manuel, a Puerto Rican, is twenty-eight years old, with dark hair, a small but strong body, and a rage that springs from drugs and hunger. He has been giving us trouble by staying in the house all afternoon and harassing everyone so we decided to restrict him to dinner. I knew there was going to be a confrontation, but I had to ask him to leave. His back was turned to me, and I was peering over his shoulder when he turned around and hit me in the jaw. A second later Michael rushed over and asked me how I was, glad that I had solved the question as to whether or not I could respond to violence in a non-violent manner. I, of course, had not even seen the punch and could not, at that point, see three feet in front of me, so I tried to smile and asked Michael for a chair to sit down. My jaw is swollen and I cannot say that I care for Manuel in the least.

I continue to take walks in the afternoon. Sometimes I go into a public library and write thoughts and poems trying to understand what this experience means to my life. I have a few friends here but I am quite lonely. Most volunteers are re-evaluating their own lives and so we share in an experience of fire and at the same time remain separated in our own worlds.

December 18

The community is filled with broken people. Few have come out of conviction, most have come out of dire need: unemployed, abandoned, outcasts. Not that the brokenness of the people here prevents moments of joy and happiness. There are moments when one laughs together with others, when one can see a common bond developing. Often, sitting on the second floor folding papers, laughter can be heard. This is a time of community, a time of sharing. But that sense of community is temporary and the volunteer is constantly called upon to renew herself/himself from within. Here the common ground is *their* ground, and mutuality, crucial for friendship, is hard to find. So the volunteer especially is alienated and without support. As referee, judge, and supposed friend, one can begin to see the difficulty of the situation. Mental tiredness is a constant feature of a volunteer's life here.

Last year when Dorothy spoke at our school I asked her whether, as Camus asked in *The Plague*, a person could be a saint without God. It seemed that she had trouble understanding the question, finally answering that without faith the Worker life was impossible. Is it possible to live a life of commitment without faith? This was the major question that brought me to the Worker.

I had been raised in a middle class neighborhood, surrounded by others of the same faith and class. Though I had been raised Jewish there was no sense that this faith had a bearing on life outside of sexual morality and preservation of the state of Israel. Nor had I been involved with the plight of the poor and the oppressed. They existed, I knew, but far from my shore. As my college years progressed, I felt an emptiness. Should I become a government worker? a professor? Could I say yes to my own career and comfort when others were homeless and broken? And if it was time to say no to things one could not believe in how did you say no? Did you say no with violence, by saying the hell with it and dropping out? Finally, if I chose a committed life what would sustain me? In the past it seemed commitment came through faith but that option did not seem viable for me.

Obviously, this question goes far beyond my person. In a world more and more devoid of faith what, in short, are the future possibilities of commitment? The Worker testament to faith jeopardizes both an affirmative answer to the question of the possibility of a saint without God, and the future of a world which acts as if God did not exist. If only self interest is to rule our world the prospects for justice seem small.

December 25
Last night I played Santa Claus for the community. I found a red vest in the clothing room and a

roll of cotton up in Michael's office. Margaret and Sharon tried to find a small present for each member of the Worker family mostly from donations. About eight o'clock we all gathered on the first floor. Thirty people showed up and a few complained about their presents. Otherwise it was nice.

This morning we fed ham and eggs to the Bowery people. The preparation was extra work but it was worthwhile. I took the house this afternoon. The atmosphere was festive. Dorothy made a rare appearance on the first floor and helped us peel potatoes for the evening meal. Hundreds of seasons greeting cards covered the walls. The light snow outside, and the warmth inside, helped create a sense of joy and community for a people without home or family.

But when Bruce, our Bowery friend, stormed in disheveled and drunk I sensed trouble. He was so loud and demanding that I had to ask him to leave. He refused, and when I became more insistent, Bruce responded by kicking me in the groin and as I doubled over, grabbing me in a headlock. From that moment I remember only that I could not breathe, and then standing apart, Bruce and I glaring at each other. Whether I struggled free or he released me, I do not know. After Bruce left I returned to my seat next to Dorothy. She whispered that during the onslaught she had prayed for me. Later when I was upstairs resting, Bruce came back and broke two windows.

December 28

Reflections on the incident with Bruce. Sharon told me that one needs, under any circumstances, to stand up and state what is right. But when Bruce returned I did not want to go outside to deter him from breaking more glass. Quite simply, I was tired and did not want to get beat up again. I questioned Sharon's statement; what good does it do to speak the truth to someone who does not understand, or is in a state where he/she cannot understand, and will only violate you for speaking the truth? What good does it do to invite physical abuse by confronting a person? Sharon pointed out that we usually rely on systemic violence (prisons, mental hospitals, run-around bureaucracies, police) to keep violence from affecting us in personal ways. Though I agree with her it seems that violence met on a pacifist level remains difficult. One cannot deal with a problem simply as an individual; the violence overwhelms you. Yet one should not create a tyranny which seems to be inherent when one delegates power. I, myself, have felt the cycle of violence ending when I refused to continue it. Rather than setting up battalions and battlefields which is what, to a large extent, our penal, police, and mental health institutions have become, one overcomes violence with love and forgiveness. The Gospel message, a scandal to be sure.

December 29

The Worker, as a Catholic lay group, attracts religiously sensitive people who, for one reason or another, have not entered formal religious life in the institutional Church. Foremost among these people is Dorothy who has lived her entire life of prayer and service as a lay Catholic. The two who interest me the most are Richard and Caryn, both of whom have been around the Worker for several years.

Richard seems to step out from the pages of a novel written by the Russian novelist Dostoevsky. He appears to be one year younger than God (though he is only fifty); he is tall and thin with a gray beard and a face which betrays an almost mystical anxiety. Years ago Richard tried to enter a religious order but was asked to leave. His life outside the order was difficult. Every two years or so he had a nervous breakdown which inevitably cost him his job. He often tells Sister Nancy that he did not choose his single status, his celibacy or his life at the Worker. He does not, however, elaborate. In the evenings Richard leads Vespers for the community. He prays much of the day and fasts often.

Caryn is twenty-six. She is talented and energetic. I would describe her also as being confused. It has not been easy for her to find a place in the world. Her life has been divided into two parts, living the life of a business executive some years ago and for the past few years a life of piety. Though she has been baptized several times in a variety of churches, Caryn insists that the only true baptism is within the Catholic Church.

Both Richard and Caryn tried to become institutional religious but were rejected. The Worker is a good community for them because it is accepting, provides an outlet for their religious feelings, lets them alone in their private expression of religiosity, and most important, sets boundaries for their public religious expression. Being surrounded by rational religious people demands that they keep in touch with reality.

December 30

There is one thing certain: the Worker is home for many people who would have no home at all. Some people who do not live here, but come everyday about four o'clock, eat dinner and leave about eight:

Rosienne, in her late forties, carries a large shopping cart filled with clothes and a thousand other items, has no home and probably sleeps in doorways, speaks English but not coherently, is kind and loving, usually kissing us good night when she leaves.

Joseph is in his fifties, stands five feet tall, is chunky and of peasant stock, speaks a combination of Russian, German, and Polish but no English except the phrase "read Bible." In a true Franciscan simplicity Joseph ties up the Worker garbage (probably about one hundred and fifty pounds worth a night) and carries it ten blocks to a park where he feeds the pigeons. He constantly prods you to read passages from the Bible out loud, then he will respond with the same reading from his Russian Bible, after which he asks you to read again. A newcomer not wanting to offend him will read the Bible to Joseph all day long!

Paul is in his seventies, stands a little under five feet, with a beautiful long gray beard (usually filled with lice). He walks the streets of New York at a snail's pace, has, like Rosienne and Joseph, no family or home, can speak two languages fluently and is senile. Paul sleeps at the municipal shelter and sometimes arrives at the Worker having been beaten up the night before.

December 31

New Year's Eve: found a man lying in the gutter unable to move, with no jacket and half-frozen. I slapped him several times, and when he came around, checked him into a flop for the night. On my way home I started to cry.

January 3

Some of us are tired of wandering
Tired of the broken hearts.
For I have seen the eyes that shine no more
Have witnessed the minds that broke after the
    winter
Sprinkled with the gentle spring.
Some of us are tired of wandering
Tired of the tears that even now well in my heart
    and soul.
For I have seen the lonely ones pacing in their
    rooms at dawn.

January 4

A peaceful day today. Louis and I talked for an hour on the second floor. I am just beginning to appreciate how much work he does around the house and how considerate he can be when he feels like it. Could it be that his rough exterior is just a front? In our own way we are becoming friends.

Helen, an older woman who lives on the third floor, mops the floors each day. She has a great sense of dignity about her. Ray also was friendly today. When he saw me overheating the tea, he scolded me gently. We both laughed about my ineptness.

January 5

At the Metropolitan Museum a painting depicting Sodom and Gomorrah. Pictured on the mountain are Lot and his children fleeing from the cities below now engulfed in flames.

January 6

Yesterday Jeff brought me a paper he was working on and asked for my comments. The paper outlined his view on Federal taxes and how these taxes were being used for military expenditures that ultimately led to war and to the death of innocents. Those opposed to the military and killing sanctified by the state, therefore, should not pay income taxes. I thought the paper was well written and told him so. He had avoided the dogmatic, and his words were a gentle plea for sanity.

Today Jeff came in with five hundred copies of the paper and asked if anyone would like to help him pass out the sheets down at the Internal Revenue Service building. Perkins remarked that in the early sixties the Worker had been alive with social protest and now the place was quiet and immersed in day to day affairs. Sharon had to take the house in the afternoon, and since I had encouraged Jeff in his writing, I thought it proper to help him in his protest.

We took a subway down and arrived at the I.R.S. building. Jeff gave me half the papers and we separated, handing them out to people on the sidewalk. As I began to pass the sheets out, I realized that my action—counseling people not to pay Federal income tax—was probably against the law. Initially, I looked upon my presence as a favor to Jeff, but as a policeman approached I was not at all sure that I wanted to be there. I had never faced a policeman like this before and for the first time I felt a vulnerability to his power. It had never occurred to me how powerful the people we pay to serve us could become when we were perceived to be in the wrong. Civil rights marchers and anti-war protestors in Chicago had found out. I had seen those events on television many steps removed. Fortunately, the policeman walked by and soon I had passed out my sheets of paper. An incident so small, though, brought to me an instant of clarification. It takes courage to stand in opposition.

January 8

Sat in the basement during soupmeal. Martin and Larry, two black fellows around fifty who have been on the Bowery for at least twenty years, came down. They stick together like a married couple; they drink together, walk together, take jobs together, quit together. Their relationship is much more than convenience. It is a deep caring relationship. Two weeks ago when Larry was stabbed at the municipal shelter, Martin came to the Worker dazed and crying. When Martin is not feeling well, Larry reacts in much the same manner.

In the afternoon a group of high school students from New Jersey came to see and learn more about the Worker. Because the first floor is noisy, we went down into the basement. There, in the stale air, with the Sermon on the Mount painted on the wall in red behind the students seated on benches, we talked about the Worker community and its vision. To the question of why a Jewish boy from Miami

80

was here in a basement off the Bowery, I could only say that it seemed the right place to be. I closed our discussion of the Worker with a verse from the Scriptures which had undergone a clarification for me in the last months:

And God said to Cain; Where is thy brother
    Abel?
And he answered: I know not. Am I my
    brother's keeper?
And God said to him: What hast thou done?
The voice of thy brother's blood crieth to me
    from the earth.

January 10

Another Friday night meeting. Michael Harrington who wrote *The Other America*, a book that helped spur Kennedy's war on poverty in the early sixties, and who lived at the Worker for a year in the fifties, came as our speaker. About thirty people attended. Harrington is a socialist and is convinced that life in the twenty-first century will be collective. Population pressures, food needs, and world inter-dependence, are some of the reasons why individual freedoms as we know them under our present system will be supplanted by systems which will put the social whole first. According to Harrington, the choice we have is whether that collectivity will be totalitarian or democratic.

The talk was interesting and provoked good discussion. As is often the case when people come from other parts of the city, our Bowery friends want to welcome them. Tonight Sharon spent most of her time keeping Bruce from smashing the windows.

81

January 12

The refusal to accept "objective" definitions of the person. The refusal, for example, to think of where we are or should be in the world of academics, or corporate hierarchy. Cut away the mystification of place, of age, of where we ought to be. The Worker exemplifies this refusal of the objective definition of the person. Here are women and men of all ages (nineteen years of age to seventy-six), working without pay, without title, dressing from donated articles, and many times doing the same tasks. Instead of status groups, the distinctions are minimal and people are accepted as equals. After forty years of life the Worker remains fluid and open most probably because of this emphasis. In short, we all do the dishes, sweep the floors, carry packages, as well as try to develop a spiritual vision. The "petty" jobs left for the "lower" classes and the technical and intellectual jobs reserved for the "upper" professional classes are combined so that an integrated person is a possibility and a sense of community rather than differentiation is achieved.

January 16

The Worker remains an alternative way of existing for the men who come in for soup. Unlike the city shelter, there are no uniforms here, no clubs or guns, just middle-class women and men who are far from imposing. Unlike the shelter there is a real attempt to treat people with dignity. At the door we greet men, "Good morning, sir." At first glance it sounds absurd. But you would be surprised how many men/women come and comment to us on why, despite the fact that the food is far less substantial here, they prefer the Worker because they are treated like human beings and not herded like animals.

Today Jim brought a man up from the basement because he pulled a knife on the person in front of him. As they got to the front door the man turned on Jim and threatened to kill him. I rushed between them and told the man to come back when he was in a better frame of mind. After he left another man got up from the table and said that he would like to talk with me. We went into the hallway and he told me that I ought to be careful what I said to the man we had just thrown out. "Yesterday," the man continued, "he cut a man's throat on the corner of Lafayette Street and left him to die." A minute later Sharon walked in and commented that I looked a little pale. I knew she wasn't kidding.

January 19

Sister Nancy and I have become good friends. Several times we have gone out to Hunts Point to beg for food for the house. Her community, Sisters of the Sacred Heart, has readily accepted me. Twice a month they invite me to their convent for dinner and conversation. Through the Worker and these sisters I am beginning to have a better insight into the religious life. Religious life is a life of discipline, denial, and order. It is a narrowing down, a creation of boundaries, a way of life. It necessitates a doing away with much external stimulus; from music to drugs to sense desire. They know the value of silence and seek a realistic freedom. I, too, am looking for a life with order and discipline.

January 22

Mary, a permanent resident of the third floor, is in her seventies, and has no family or means of support. She has large open sores on her back that she rebandages three times a day, but refuses medical care. She collects clothes from the clothing room and from the streets (her room is forcibly cleaned out once a year), and rarely sleeps at night. Most would insist that Mary be put in a nursing home where her ailments would be treated and she would be taken care of properly by "professionals." But here she has life; not a round of bridge and a game of checkers, but freedom and a community which challenges her faculties. Thoughts of Mary and the soupmeal when reading the May issue of the *Catholic Worker* which lists the Worker's positions:

We advocate a complete rejection of the present social order and a non-violent revolution to establish an order more in accord with Christian values. This can only be done by direct action since political means have failed as a method for bringing about this society. Therefore we advocate a personalism which takes upon ourselves responsibility for changing conditions to the extent that we are able to do so. By establishing Houses of Hospitality we can take care of as many of those in need as we can rather than turn them over to the impersonal charity of the State. We do not do this in order to patch up the wrecks of the capitalist system but rather because there is always a shared responsibility in these things and a call

84

to minister to our brother and sister transcends any consideration of economics.

January 25

Margaret showed me an article today originally written in 1950 by William Gauchat entitled "Voluntary Poverty; Way of Freedom."

Voluntary poverty, being the means that removes the obstacles which stand in the way of spiritual perfection, which is love, is primarily the most potent means of preserving justice, without which love is impossible. It is a positive means of not being directly or indirectly guilty of injustice to our neighbor, the worker, the teeming multitudes slaving on below subsistence levels who produce the raw materials for modernity's inflated wants. It relieves us of the responsibility of being silent partners, or minority stockholders in enterprises for draining the lifeblood of workers to fill an insatiable avarice.

The article is interesting because it links simplicity of life (or the deflating of our material desires) with the question of justice. Simply put, factories with their assembly lines are not conducive for healthy human beings. By demanding more and more material goods we assure the continuance and growth of these factories. Voluntary poverty, when looked at in this light, is not only being with those who are deprived but also protesting against de-humanizing labor. Is it just for us to accept material goods that come at such a high human cost?

January 27

Peter is a fifth floor resident. Seven months ago a volunteer found him in a park, beaten up, hungry, and broke, and brought him to the Worker. He has been here ever since. Peter will be fifty in March, is intelligent (with an M.A. in English from the University of Iowa), writes good poetry, and considers himself to be a radical. Right now he is on the waiting list to be called as a substitute teacher in the New York public school system.

His life story is interesting. Estranged from his family, Peter has never married, and is a convert to Catholicism. In the late forties he went to Israel and since then has traveled to Europe several times. In 1968 Peter went to France with a group of people to set up a United States government in exile in protest over our involvement in the Vietnam war. He claims that the C.I.A. has hounded him ever since, isolating him from his friends, shutting off all job opportunities, and driving him to the brink of suicide. Peter has described to me two of his suicide attempts.

I wonder about him quite a lot. His moods change so rapidly. He hates being among "bums" and thinks that by providing food and hospitality for Bowery people we are encouraging a type of life which Peter considers uncivilized. On the other hand, after speaking with Steve or Sharon, he will express to me his amazement at their depth of compassion. His moods cause many verbal confrontations that escalate into fights. At night, especially when Ray insists that lights be out, Peter does not comply. A week ago at one in the morning I found both of them squaring off right in front of my bed. Half asleep, I scrambled in between them. It is a wonder someone was not killed.

February 1

Last night I walked Perkins to his hotel in the Bowery. The streets were crowded with people, some lying on the ground and others walking, drinking cheap liquor. Men were wandering in the middle of the road asking drivers in stopped cars for money. The temperature was thirty-five degrees and the profound misery of the Bowery people could be seen. It is hard to explain this misery: no home, no proper diet, no accessible toilets, little change of clothing, the need to walk the streets all day and night, the necessity to drink in order to deaden the pain.

February 5

Steve has awakened in me, once again, the need to express the nature of the volunteers here, especially Steve, Sharon, and Margaret. The depth of their compassion, the greatness of their humility, their unannounced faith that speaks in a vision as well as in day to day affairs is hard to describe. They are the most unpretentious, but most thoroughly tested Christians possible. I have said it before but it needs to be said over and over again: they live the Gospel.

Their depth of love and understanding continues to challenge my "hardness" of heart. I have been getting shorter and shorter with people, less and less tolerant of others, more and more exclusive. While I see this, I am having little success in changing my course. These six months have introduced me to a new world of poverty, of broken lives, to new thoughts of what my place ought to be in a world filled with the oppressed.

And what ought to be my place (the place of the privileged) in a world filled with the oppressed? This, I suppose, is the perennial question, the question, perhaps, which forms the very heart of the Sermon on the Mount. One can hardly escape the feeling that this is the central question of our century also. It is, above all, a question that I have preferred to ask in the abstract surrounded by family and friends. But for me now, the question has been raised by the bodies and souls of those who suffer. (Has the answer been posed by those who serve?) And I cannot help feeling, in the midst of this tension and anger, that I have been led to a place which is, at the same moment, a desert and the promise of a garden. "And after this our exile" (Eliot).

February 8

In the morning,
Amidst the dreams and the loneliness,

Lodged

Between the rocks and the waters

Wrapped

In a subconscious frenzy
(That is, despite its nature, repetitive),
The sorrow comes to rest.

In the morning
The sorrow loses its many faces
And becomes what it cannot escape:
The quiet separation.

February 10

Today Father Dan Berrigan gave a day of recollec-
tion for Worker volunteers. Margaret told me that
Dan is extremely fond of the Worker, is a friend of
Dorothy's and has celebrated Mass at the Worker on
many occasions. I had only heard about Dan as a
Jesuit priest who continually protested the war in
Vietnam and had gone to jail several times for his
protest. As we traveled downtown on the subway to
his home I wondered what he would be like as a
person. I was anxious about meeting him. I extended my hand but instead of shaking my hand he
embraced me.

The day was very informal. We began with forty-
five minutes of meditation; then we had Mass. Dan
said Mass differently than most I had attended before; the order of the Mass was sometimes reversed
and several petitions were extended. The homily
was shared, volunteers and Dan alternately contri-
buting thoughts and ideas.

The main theme of the homily was a search for
the meaning of the Book of Revelation, the great
apocalyptic book of the New Testament. For Dan
the Scripture pointed to the destruction of our
present society, a total rending of life as we know
it. Different views emerged but the destruction of
present reality seemed to be the consensus. Need-
less to say, the atmosphere was gloomy. I was silent.
I could not help hoping that in some way our society

89

would not be destroyed—there was too much blood and death in the destruction for me—but would somehow be reconciled with the needs of the people. It was, I know, a vague thought, one that I could not articulate there. But the image of reconciliation stayed inside me and before me. Like the pillar of light for the Jews in the desert it would not go away.

Spending time with someone like Dan is not simply a personal encounter but a learning experience as well. Being with Dorothy is very similar. Here are two radicals, both living a thoroughly committed life, both in opposition to the present system, both speaking out and willing to go to prison for their thoughts and actions. They seem so fearless you might expect them to be hard and cold. They meet thousands of people each year so you might think that they would be indifferent to you as a person. The opposite is true. What makes Dan and Dorothy so amazing is that they are filled with love, not just for God or humankind but for persons as they are. When I think about Dan and Dorothy and what they stand for, they seem rather special.

February 12

Christine is sixty-one years old. She is a large woman, spry for her age, with long black hair, and speaks with a mid-western accent. She has lived on the third floor in the big room for the past year. Her arguments with Mary are long and continuous. Mary is a collector. Her room, which is set off by a large curtain, is bulging with items she has collected from the street. Christine, on the other hand, keeps her area immaculate. To Christine, Mary is filthy, so there are constant arguments over how much junk is in Mary's room and what sides of the big room she is using. Of course the bickering is not confined to their floor; each day there is a confrontation between Christine and Mary on the first floor also.

Christine, being more agile and energetic, enlists support from the regulars who stay in during the afternoon. When Mary comes down around four to get her supper, which invariably includes fingering the bread and looking into the stove, Christine and those she has enlisted on her side begin their cat calls. If you can imagine Mary shuffling quietly on her rounds, and the abuse she takes ("Rotten bum," "Filthy bitch,") added to three more voices telling me to stop her from touching the food, you can begin to understand the noise levels that are typical and predictable every day.

There is so much pettiness. It is rumored Christine receives money from outside sources and pays little to the Worker for her room and board. She has no expenses; she simply accumulates the money. Every other day, though, she takes thirty Worker newspapers to Union Square and sells them. How much she sells them for no one knows but we are sure it is not for a penny a copy! With all of that, she demands fifty cents a night from house money. The person taking the house is given about five dollars a night to dispense to those in need and it has become traditional to give Christine her fifty cents. Last night, when I had the house, she demanded seventy-five cents. I asked her why the raise, and, as I reached into my pocket for the money, it turned out that I had only thirty-five cents left. Earlier I had paid for a man into a flop for the night and I was short of money. I told her that I was sorry, explained to her the circumstances, and offered her the thirty-five cents I had. She became angry and knocked the money from my hand. Christine started yelling, "You cheap son of a bitch. . . . You dirty rotten son of a bitch. . . . Who do you think you are you young punk?" I walked away but she kept following me for the next hour berating my intellect, my morals, and my virility.

Today the battle continued. Christine spent the entire day telling everyone the "truth" about me. She never let up not even for an instant. When I walked in for dinner she followed me around, spitting at me, and using every invective in the book. Soon others, who had been my friends the day before, joined the chorus. I left my plate sitting on the table and walked outside. We were quibbling over nickels and dimes but the conflict went much deeper. To meet emergencies we were given five dollars a night. If a man stumbles to the door and needs a flop what am I to do, tell him: "Sorry Christine needs her seventy-five cents"?

February 13

Same thing today. Christine will not leave me alone. The volunteers all agree with me. Christine can have her fifty cents a night but no more, and if someone is in greater need then the money goes to the person in greater need, period. But though the volunteers agree with me in principle, they continue to give her the money she asks for. To me it is a question of justice; others in the community receive nothing at all each day from house funds but because Christine is loud and threatening she re-

92

ceives. Why can't we have consistent policy on the matter? The abuse is getting worse and the tension inside the house is something fierce. I told Sharon today that until I received some tangible support from the volunteers I would not take the house again.

As I walked up the stairs to my bed on the fifth floor I felt alone. It was all so brutal. The walls were an institutional brown and the paint was peeling. On each floor a door led you to, what appeared to be, a fixed reality. Nothing seemed to move or become different. The second floor would be full of people folding and labeling newspapers — full of the same people with the same discussions and arguments day after day. Beyond the third floor door were Christine and Mary, and three or four others who always took on supporting roles in their continuing drama. The fourth floor had the permanent men, older men sleeping in a dormitory, lonely men who might die in their beds during the night. And the fifth floor, my home, seemed little better. The petty bickering, the unmade beds, the lockers that lined the walls and would not close.

When I reached the fifth floor I knew what I would see before I opened the door. Peter would be typing his poetry, Don would be sleeping, Robert would be drunk, reading his newspapers, and cussing underneath his breath, and a new fellow Mike, would be half-clothed with a head full of lice lying on his bed staring at the wall. No one looked up as I entered the room. Peter, who was between sentences, stared at his sheet of paper in the typewriter and asked affectionately, "How you doing kid?"

Living, working, and eating here is a total way of

life. For the first few months living in the house is essential. Without being thrown into the life here it would be difficult to cope with any part of Worker life. You would be an alien presence to the people and would be unable to understand what was going on. But after five months or so it is important to move to an apartment so you can get some space, some area where you can be by yourself and reflect. Otherwise, you can become a prisoner. Margaret has mentioned something about a room in a building (a former music school) the Worker has acquired in order to transform it into a home for abandoned women. I need to ask her more about the possibility.

February 14

Thinking about the last few days I am struck by my judgments and assumptions. Am I being fair to Christine? Does she have money put aside? Who knows? I wonder if it matters anyway. She has a need to be here just as I, in my own way, am in need. That beautiful quote from *Diary of a Country Priest*: "How little we know what a human life really is—even our own. To judge us by what we call our actions is probably as futile as to judge us by our dreams." I do not know her and yet I judge.

February 15

Reflections on the desert.

The desert stands barren always behind us, stretches out quietly always to meet us. In the desert one is a wanderer, if blessed with purpose, a pilgrim. But there are no homes here, only nomads. Many who come to the desert have been ripped away, driven with lash into the heat. Others come willingly in response to a calling.

There is little to recommend life in the desert; only the sun and the stars and the sand to keep one company. In the desert loneliness is a way of life. The desert is an infinity of sand and heat with no beginning, no end, only the silence and perpetual surrender. There is no history in the desert; no milestones or fame. There are no castles to build in the desert because there are no eyes. There are no strangers because all are strangers even the tribe. And home is just a moment, a tent, to be moved away and traveled over at the morning dawn. The desert is a place of movement where nothing moves; an infinity of time in a timeless world. The desert is the silent ground where progression and action and meaning die and are buried. There are no markers in the desert, no burial grounds for the rich or religious that do not, in a short time, become particles of sand, blending, indistinguishable. The desert consumes all that is artificial. Only the moment remains and that is quickly consumed in heat and the desire to die.

And yet the mirage is born in the desert; reminding us of possibility, promising peace, refreshment, renewal. The desert, for all its barrenness, gives rise to the oasis. The desert demands thirst. The oasis offers water from underground. The desert consumes energy with heat. The oasis offers shade and rejuvenation. The desert makes barren all the human eye can see. The oasis refreshes the eye with greenery and livable space. The desert poses all questions. The oasis answers but for a moment only.

Because the oasis gives it is destined to be consumed. Because it offers solace it is by nature used and abused. It is this very life that brings the oasis back to the desert and death. The oasis is but a moment in a long death. Once again the answer fades away and only the burning question, the desert, remains.

February 18

Gene has been planning to leave for several months. Tomorrow he will finally depart. He has been at the Worker for four years, and because of his intelligence and dedication to Worker life, has become one of the major people here. I never really got to know him well; Gene was busy editing the paper and worked daily in the house as well. Because most all of the volunteers looked up to him, Gene's departure leaves a great gap here at the house. But the work goes on. Margaret will be moving into the apartment tomorrow and will assume the position of editor of the paper. She has invited me to come over to her apartment and spend the afternoon.

The winter is so hard on the poor. Landlords control the heat in the apartments and, often as not, the heat is off altogether. Street people are in the worst shape. Those who have flops for the night are expected to be out by seven in the morning and cannot return until six in the evening. Many of our friends spend the entire day moving about in order not to freeze. All over the Lower East Side the scene is familiar.

Jim and Alberto are away for a few days and I am the only volunteer on the fifth floor. Because they are away we have an extra bed. Last night a young black fellow, Quincy, came by looking for a place to stay. I told him we had an empty bed and that he was welcome. This morning Raymond, who also sleeps in the big room, accused Quincy of making homosexual advances to him during the night. Raymond demanded that Quincy be forced to leave. I talked to Quincy and told him that he was to remain in his own bed during the night and should begin to look for another place to stay. Raymond was furious that I allowed him to remain at the Worker. I told him that Quincy had no money and no place to sleep. My decision was final.

February 20

Two o'clock in the afternoon. I am sitting in Margaret's living room looking out across the street. The temperature is in the low thirties. Three young men stand in front of the Worker. None is older than thirty. All are badly dressed; one has no coat. Jim has the house and is letting people in selectively. Because the men drink heavily in winter to keep warm, there have been a number of fights on the first floor in the last few days. Jim is being careful.

A woman walks out on the street. She is wearing high heeled shoes, with short red pants and a long army coat unbuttoned down the front. A man walks up to the door and rings the bell. He is dressed in a suit and is straightening the knot of his tie as he waits for the door to open. But his suit is old and crumpled (too short in the legs and in the sleeves) and he is twitching continually as if in a mild seizure. A black man walks toward the door, stops and leans against the building to keep his balance. He is wearing a crumpled postal uniform.

Jim opens the door and tells the men that they cannot come in now. One man grabs the door and tries to wrestle control from Jim. The door finally slams shut. Another man hurls his fist against the plastic window in the door. It is going to be a long day.

It is so quiet in here, relatively warm and secure. I cannot help but wonder what drives a person to the Bowery. Is it a lost love, a family tragedy, a mental aberration? After a while you begin to wonder why you are in the apartment and they are on the street. Last night I dreamt that I opened the door in the morning and my father was waiting outside in the line. I walked up to him and asked him what he was doing here. He said he was hungry.

February 23

Walked Perkins to a hotel on the Bowery. As I was walking back I heard three piercing cries for help. Across the street I saw a group of men standing over a person. A man's body was moving back and forth and I thought it might be a rape. I wanted to help but was frightened. Some of the men probably had guns; knives were a certainty. A few seconds later I started across the street having no idea what I would do when I reached the men. As I started across I saw a man pulling up his pants and the pack starting to move on. Another man lay sprawled on the sidewalk. It was fairly dark over there so I called out to see if he was all right. He pulled himself up and waved me away. I hurried home.

February 24

Reflections on the exile

In the deepest reaches of man's psyche, in the beginning of humankind's mythical history, lies exile. With exile comes the definition of what it means to be human. Exile, in the expulsion of Adam, signals the beginning of time, of division, of multiple levels of reality. Exile is the end of infinity, the inheritance of moment. It is the loss of innocence. In exile we perceive our nakedness. Exile, too, is the tasting of death, the severed connection between humankind and God, and so becomes the essence of fear. Exile is the loss of home, and security, and place. It is the beginning of the perpetual wandering.

Exile is the expulsion of Eve, the appearance of pain and of condemnation. It is the perception of otherness, of separation, and distrust. Exile, at its very roots, becomes a struggle for physical and psychic survival and thus demands a distinction between the human and nature. Its hand is in the beginnings of the desire to conquer and the terror of risk. Exile spells the end of illusion and omnipotence. It is the tossing out into a world of uncertainty and danger and darkness. And when even the sworded cherubim disappears, exile is the beginning of loneliness.

February 25

The former music school which the Worker is going to renovate to create a home for abandoned women is to be called Mary House. I received word from Michael that someone was needed to watch the building at night. I said that I would be glad to take on the job, and my plans are to move over there in a week or so.

Mary House is on East Third Street just two blocks from the First Street house. The building is huge; four stories high and the width of two brownstones. It cost $110,000.00 to buy—all of which was donated by a monastery. Renovation will cost as much as the purchase price. Where are we going to get the money I ask Michael? "If it is God's will, the way will be provided."

My room will be on the third floor. The paint is flaking and there is a little graffiti on the wall but a few post cards hung in the right places and a bed will make it a paradise for me.

Eighty thousand *Catholic Worker* newspapers were delivered to the house today for folding and labeling. All are wrapped in bundles and each bundle contains two hundred-fifty newspapers. The papers have to be transported from the truck (which we rent for the day) up to the second floor. A line stretching from the truck up the stairs to the second floor is formed, and bundles are passed from one person to another. The work is tiring. Volunteers, as well as people from the house, pitch in. Sometimes a Bowery person, after finishing his soupmeal, joins the line. This delivery represents one of the few times when a number of us work together as a group. When people get tired and drop out of the line gaps develop and the load becomes heavier, especially when you have to walk upstairs to reach the next person. There is a wealth of labor on the first floor but no one is asked to help. Personal initiative only; not even a gentle coercion is allowed.

Emily is a new volunteer. She is a few years older than I am, is intelligent, and has developed, in her short stay here, a good rapport with the people in the house. Her parents live in Connecticut and she has invited me up to her family's home for three days. It will be a welcome rest.

February 27

Notes on the ride to Stamford, Connecticut. Staring out the window. The alley is cold, forbidding, empty of people. Only two filled garbage cans without tops stand in the rain. Broken glass and four cats winding through the alley looking for food. Winter is bleak in the city.

The street is quiet. Few cars in the early morning. One lone tree, in a square cut from the sidewalk, stands bare. The tree is thin, undernourished, naked. The buildings are old and neglected. Many of the windows are broken, unfixed for months. The street is dark. Desolation.

The highway is wide, definite. Cutting through the hills and the grasslands without deference and with ease. Inside a silent journey, watching the country roll by, alone without words or crowding. The dawn breaks. Day lies ahead. One thinks on a journey of those things past, and what the future might become. Between the places—coming from and going to—lies a peaceful hope. Not a longing but a quiet hour. Thinking of the faces that make the journey soft, the winter becomes simply a moment of transition waiting for the deliverance of spring.

February 28

The countryside is so beautiful, the rolling hills and the fences made of stones. Clean air! Today I saw some horses and a few cows. The house is so quiet and I am eating meals with only three other people. Amazing. How different everything is here.

Out of the silence
came Jesus the Word,
In the confusion of division and diversity
came Jesus the unity.

I was walking in the desert (weren't you?)
And there in the distance
in the haze and mists of desert life
stood Jesus the healer.
He was
        preaching to the rocks
        singing to the winds
He was
        creating the loaves
        multiplying the softness
He was
        gazing out into the distance
        talking to the clouds
He was
        feeling the roundness of the earth
        at peace crying.

March 1

Tonight we return to New York. I have tried to free myself from the Worker and simply enjoy the country. As usual, however, Emily and I have thought and talked of little else but the Worker. The experience is so encompassing that getting away mentally is difficult. Emily, who is living on the third floor and cooking in the afternoons, has a whole set of stories I have not heard. We exchange laughs and sometimes a few tears.

I am trying to gain perspective on my journey at the Worker. It seems that I am finally being accepted by the community itself. Those who live and work at the house, as well as the street people, really put you through a period of testing until they realize you are determined to stick with your work and survive. Then all of a sudden you are doing things right instead of wrong. It was so difficult for me to accept the community as it was. Like every new person I tried to change things. But the reality of the Worker overpowers you and soon toleration replaces the desire to change. Knowing your limits is your life jacket here. I think also that I am becoming closer with some of the volunteers. Perhaps I have earned their friendship. I am looking forward to my own room when I return.

March 3

The heat at Mary House is off again. Fortunately, I found a set of thermal underwear in the clothing room. I scavenged up a bed and a set of dresser drawers today from the second floor. I finished my room decorations by going down to the Metropolitan Museum of Art and purchasing some cheap reproductions. For four dollars I have ten of the greatest paintings in history hanging on my walls.

The winter brings many fires to the Lower East Side. Inadequate wiring and faulty gas lines plague the apartment buildings in which the poor are forced to live. In the early hours of the morning I hear the fire trucks' sirens and horns. Sometimes when the fire is close I can hear the fire people smashing windows with their axes. Otherwise my room is rather quiet. Tomorrow I will look for a desk.

Soup is a constant at the Worker. Two pots of soup are prepared each morning, one for the soupmeal and one for the community's lunch. For seven months now I have been eating soup for lunch almost every day. The soup is completely homemade; fresh vegetables and beans are cut up and boiled down in the early morning. Presently there are three soup makers, each with her own distinctive style. On our lucky days, we have day-old bread donated by Macy's international bakery which means Russian black bread and good French bread. When the soup is good and the donation is there, lunch can be superb.

March 5

This afternoon I took the house. Lunch went smoothly. At one o'clock the first floor was relatively empty. Sister Nancy was getting ready for the evening meal. Emily had gone to the butcher to buy meat. The buzzer rang and I went to the door. Jody was standing outside. There are several people here whom I am afraid of but he frightens me more than anyone. Under no circumstances is Jody to get inside. He is simply too dangerous. I signalled Jody to move away from the door and told him I would come out and talk with him if he did. He moved a step back. I took a deep breath, opened the door, stepped outside, and began to close the door behind me. As I was closing the door, Jody drew out a knife and told me that if the door closed behind me he was going to slit my throat. Before I realized it the door was closed and we were standing outside face to face. Jody was heavily drugged. I tried to make a joke out of his threat. I told him I was not worth a couple of years in prison. He laughed. It was cold outside but I could feel perspiration running down my face. Jody started talking about Melville's *Moby Dick* and then about Hawthorne's *The Scarlet Letter*. He asked me if I knew anything about the symbolism in the books and I replied that I knew very little about the subject. Midway through his analysis of early American literature he slipped his knife into his coat pocket. Fifteen minutes went by and I told Jody I had some work to do. He said he understood, that I was a good kid, and left. I opened the door and sat down inside. I prayed that I would never see that man again.

March 6

The heat in my new home has been off for three days. Sharon invited me to stay over in her apartment for a few days.

Sharon's apartment has two rooms and a bathroom. The front room is used as a bedroom, a living room, and a kitchen. The second room is a "Christ" room where guests are welcome. Sharon constantly takes people in, sometimes even families. There is little natural light in the apartment. All her windows open out to brick walls. Dishes are piled up in the sink and the dining room table is filled with papers and used tea bags. The beds are on the floor. She has no telephone.

I have been awake for a few minutes. Someone is knocking at the door. Sharon is out of bed answering the door. A friend named Patrick, who is strung out on speed, needs to speak with her. Patrick is welcomed and eases into a chair at the table. She offers him a cup of tea as he rattles off ten or fifteen events that have taken place since he came by last. The stories are disjointed. Patrick is tired. He has bags under his eyes that are heavy and discolored. His face is pale. Sharon looks tired too. She tries to lighten his feeling of being "screwed over," and does this by joking with him, all the while showing care for his confusion. For volunteers who have been here for a year or two, living among the poor outside the Worker house is part of their commitment. Those in need are rarely, if ever, turned away.

I am glad that Sharon does not have a phone. Yesterday, when I had the house, I must have answered the phone a thousand times. Most calls were requests either to speak with someone who was not in the house (but you have to look and make sure she/he is not in a corner somewhere) or to provide food and lodging for people in need. Requests for food and lodging invariably come from Catholic Charities or city welfare agencies. We are so very small yet we are first on their list to phone. Worse than the phone calls, however, are the people who arrive at our front door at ten o'clock in the evening with a slip from an agency asking if they can have a bed for the night. Last night it was a mother and a young daughter.

March 7

Temperature was in the fifties today. A pleasant change. The sun was shining and I took a walk to

106

Washington Square. On my way I was stopped four times by Bowery people to chat for a few minutes. First time was by Dale who hangs out underneath a marquis on Fourth Street. Then on Sixth Street by Joan who was wearing an array of buttons on her blouse, and carrying a whiskey flask in her pocket. Later, crossing Bleeker Street I was stopped by three men who recognized me from the soupmeal, and finally, as I headed into Washington Square, another comrade shook my hand and walked on by.

It brought back a memory that makes me chuckle. A week ago I went to see Harold and Maude at the St. Mark's Theater. It is close to the Worker and just one dollar for two features. Whenever I want to change "worlds," as it were, I go to see a movie. The price is low and the theater is warm so a number of Bowery people frequent the theater in the afternoon. As I sat down I noticed a man, whom I recognized from the soupmeal, sitting two rows in front of me. His hair was very long and he was picking lice off his coat. To the left of me another man slumped in his seat and as his arm fell to his side a wine flask was knocked out of his pocket onto the floor. I sighed to myself, vowed never to return to the St. Mark's, and proceeded to enjoy the film.

March 10

Mass tonight was a combination of reverence and humor. You never quite know what is going to happen at any given point of the Mass. A week ago Will smashed a window during the Our Father. Tonight the intentions offered were the highlight. Everyone is quiet. A prayer is offered for a friend who is suffering from cancer. Silence again. Lester, an old time Worker, offers a prayer for the defeat of "god-

107

less communism" and the victory of "Mother Church" in Russia. Margaret smiles. Ralph, who feels he is being mistreated by Michael, offers a prayer for the repose of Michael's soul. Michael is sitting in the front row. Joan comes up from the basement and staggers down the aisle complaining that Ruth (who sleeps in the basement with Joan) is a pig and a thief. Louis stands in the hallway muttering about those "saintly hypocrites" who go to Mass, and then reacts to Joan in his usual manner, "Come on lady, if you want to get drunk, get the hell out of here before I belt you." Jeff walks over to try to calm Louis down before he and Joan go at it. Sharon is chuckling. Mass, of course, goes on.

It is strange when I reflect that the words God and Jesus are heard at the Worker only at Mass and Vespers. No grace is said, and no counsel is offered. Even when you are interested in the role God plays in the volunteers' lives, there is a great reticence to discuss it. There is never a distinction drawn between who is a Catholic or non-Catholic, a believer or a non-believer. The question is never raised.

Part of my problem in relation to God, I am sure, is the way the term itself was used in my religious education. God the Mighty King, God the Pillar of Life, God, God, God. When you asked who God was, there was a categorical answer: God is. . . . Around you, though knowing who God was made little difference in the way people lived. The belief did not noticeably increase one's love or one's concern. In the speaking and defining of the word God, the efficacy and the spirit were lost.

Here there is no speech, no definition of character, no easy answer to who God is and what he does. Sometimes you feel God emerging from and merging into the experience of service. Perhaps it is in service that the spirit is found. It is not, to be sure, a large and bold God, but a subtle one. Sometimes you feel a presence suffering here with you and the others. Sometimes you feel a body being broken. At other times you feel yourself surrounded by grace.

March 11

A failure hangs crucified
The field account verifies the abortion

Here

In the twilight
Confronting, as it were,
The evening hours with death
And dawn with the Word and the silence

Here

In the twilight
Dividing two worlds
I would approach his side with a doubt and a
    smile
If his procession had not surrounded mine
    with ashes
And left a lonely voice to survive and to testify

Here

In the twilight
Dividing two worlds
(Pointing somehow to a joining)
It is not enough to be a victim.

March 12

Ten people have arrived from a Catholic college in Minnesota to live at the Worker for a week. They will stay at Mary House with me. Accommodations are sparse; one bathroom to a floor and two beds. Fortunately, most brought sleeping bags. In the morning they worked the soupmeal and in the afternoon they helped take broken tiles and rotted wood outside to the garbage. Tomorrow they will sweep and start to scrape the floors clean of old wax. There is so much work that needs to be done here; painting, scraping, and cleaning are only the beginnings. Most of this work will be done by volunteers who come in groups and stay for a week or ten days.

They are a very jovial group, even to the point of kidding around and singing a song during the soupmeal today. I have to admit that this "joy" repulses me. Serving people, who have been broken by life, with a song offends any sense of the real situation. Perhaps they are nervous being here, and this is the only way they can handle what they see. Everyone is awkward when he/she arrives because the situation is unimaginable. I talked to Steve about the "song" today. We agreed that a certain gaiety was offensive here. I must try to be patient.

March 13

A group of sisters came to the Worker to visit. Dorothy was up on the third floor and came down to talk with them. I had the house and the afternoon was fairly quiet.

Dorothy was very interested in the sisters and insisted that they tell her what work they were engaged in and what their interests were. The sisters were beginning a small community on the land and Dorothy wanted to know what crops they planned to plant and what animals they hoped to raise. They told Dorothy that they had been greatly influenced by her witness. Dorothy quickly launched into a discussion of Peter Maurin's principles, his vision of a life on the land and the learning of crafts. She spent about an hour with the sisters, telling of her various experiences with Catholic Worker farms, and then grew weary. She kissed each one of them, told them to keep in touch, and started for the stairs. She called me over and asked me how I was doing. I smiled and said, "Fine." She patted my arm, then turned and began the climb to her room on the third floor.

March 14

An hour before dinner, people begin gathering on the first floor. Paul, of course, has been here all afternoon. His beard is full of lice as is his clothing. Between scratches, Paul has been taking coffee cups from the table one by one, and putting them into his bag. He moves so slowly that catching him in the act of taking the cups is not difficult. Still, though caught depositing a cup in his bag, Paul vehemently denies any wrong doing. When the table needs to be set for dinner, you have to take his bag into the bathroom and remove the cups he has taken. First, however, you must sort through the silverware and the food he has scavenged from garbage cans.

George is in from the backyard where he has worked all day tying up garbage and keeping the patio clean. Joseph has just delivered food to the pigeons and is asking people to "read Bible, read Bible." Big Mike arrives. Neither Joseph nor Big Mike speak much English but that does not dampen their desire to communicate their wishes and frustrations in their native tongues.

Emily is cooking. Pots are boiling and the noise in the room is rising. The problem is that each one of the four o'clock crowd talks to the other and out loud to himself/herself. Then George gets on Joseph for something, Big Mike agrees (in Polish of course) and the roundtable begins. Dinner is a relief.

On the second floor, there is a small library tucked away in the room that holds the address files of people who receive the Worker newspaper. At night the room is empty and often I browse through the books for a couple of hours. The books reflect the philosophy of the Worker itself. Books by Thomas Merton and Mahatma Gandhi are numerous as well as the lives of the saints like St. John of the Cross and St. Theresa.

A book entitled *The Awakening* by Kate Chopin struck my eye tonight and I read it. The major character is a wealthy Louisiana woman, married and with children, who embarks on a quest to find her own identity in the society of the 1890's. The theme is the liberation of a strong woman who is searching for life and meaning. Literature so rarely presents a woman searching and strong that I was surprised to find even this one book.

Women at the Worker, from the beginning with Dorothy, now with Sharon, Margaret, and Emily, and into the future with the coming of Mary House which will be fully staffed by women, carry much of the burden of the Worker movement on their shoulders. These are women who in the very living of their lives search out and pursue paths of liberation. It is not, to be sure, a celebration of the *appetites* but a liberation through trial and service drawn from an ascetic life of sacrifice and love.

This life of living and working among the poor and the destitute elicits a certain strength of character that is not easily described. Conceivably, it is difficult to describe because our societal image of women is so different from what women at the Worker have become. Here women do not dress for men, or make men the center of their lives. Attraction is not the basis of life, or even a peripheral concern. It is values and ideas which form the focal point of their life. Their strength of character comes from having plunged into living life rather than having been protected from it, from risking the role they were raised to fill, and striking out into the reality of suffering.

March 15

The fall appeal for donations, sent out in November, is still bringing in checks from all over the country. This year donations will probably reach $100,000.00. All will be spent serving the poor and by fall of next year the Worker will be broke and asking for support again. Most of the donations are small; ten, fifteen and twenty-five dollar checks are typical.

The majority of donations come through the mail and the volume of mail is staggering. In January, volunteers start taking home handfuls of mail and

113

writing thank yous to each contributor. Not only is each contribution acknowledged; a letter often accompanies the donation, and that letter is also answered. The process takes months but the Worker revolves around a personal approach that would not allow a general reply in the paper or an impersonal word of appreciation in the mail.

Aside from donations, many other letters are received by the Worker each day. People who are praying for the house of hospitality, people who are expressing an indebtedness to the Worker's witness, and many who are either announcing a venture of their own, or asking advice on how to start a farm or a soup kitchen, make up the bulk of the mail. Dorothy's mail is a phenomenon in itself and she tends to it personally as much as she can.

Mail is extremely important to members of the community. Michael's office is besieged each morning when the mail is delivered. The prospect of receiving mail gives the people somewhere to be at ten every morning. Most go away empty handed.

We receive donations other than money. Tonight about eight o'clock a man drove up in a station wagon filled with dairy products. Their "to be sold by" date had passed and he could no longer sell them to his customers. He asked if we could use the food. We now have fifty cartons of cottage cheese and ten cheese spreads in our refrigerator. A few weeks ago a man drove up in a van and asked if we needed some food. He had just catered a birthday party and the leftover food was going to be thrown away. The next day at lunch we served stuffed cabbage, Italian salad, and some beautiful chopped liver.

Clothes are also donated. People come by and leave a box of old clothing, or sometimes bring a single item like a pair of shoes or a winter coat.

March 17

Since I came back from Connecticut, it has become more and more difficult for me to tell people what to do. When you have the house everyone appeals to your judgment. Can I do this? Should I go here? What should I do about this? Actually, I would like very much to come into the Worker and leave it without saying a word or directing an action. I really seek silence. I would like to become gentle again.

Sharon came over to Third Street and talked with me. We talked about the Worker, about our volunteer status, and the consequences of that status. I told her about my desire for peace and spoke of the burdensome nature of the volunteer's responsibility. Her deep compassion makes it impossible to intellectualize matters around her. Sharon brings everything down to earth. We talked of the loneliness of people like Bruce and our own loneliness. She put forth the idea that loneliness appears and takes hold out of a desire for God. We talked about love and she commented that most people looked for fulfillment in others and that this was impossible. Margaret made a statement about popular music a while ago along the same lines. She said that most popular songs revolve around a lost person looking for a savior in another person. For her, though, the dimension which made love for others important and possible was God.

Sharon made another interesting distinction

which I need to reflect on. She said that for her the religious question was not one of denominations and different traditions but whether one affirmed a material or a spiritual reality. For here there are two prisons, the prison of material goods and the prison of culture.

March 18

Like any culture, ours provides us with a certain world view, a set of understandings about the human being and social systems. We are told, for instance, that our economic system is the best in the world, or that our nuclear warheads are for our own protection. Being with the poor and the destitute challenges these understandings. If twenty-five million Americans are defined as poor by government estimates and another fifteen million hover right on the edge of poverty, whom does our economic system serve? If our military systems are geared toward total destruction do they, in the end, protect us or put us in more and more danger?

Sharon and other volunteers question these cultural assumptions. They ask: Is this the way we ought to live? Is this the way others should have to live? This questioning of assumptions comes through their commitment to the poor and their religious faith. Here the Church is not supporting our culture but profoundly questioning it, not blowing our assumptions up in smoke, but stripping them bare.

The continuity of the Worker commitment can be traced by perusing back issues of the Worker newspaper. Beginning in 1933 the issues catalogue the concerns of Worker people over the years. Supporting labor unions, (with an eye toward the dignity of labor as much as material advancement), championing black and Indian rights, forseeing the gathering storms of war and organizing against it, arguing for decentralized village economies, and caring for the poor and the oppressed, all are themes that were treated in *Catholic Worker* during 1933 as well as 1975.

The early years, especially, called forth a style of writing which was both excellent in content and remarkably energetic. Looking back, though, the most striking quality of the newspaper is its ability to see through social and political propaganda, and present viable alternatives to harmful thoughts and actions. As early as 1934, for example, the Worker predicted the coming of World War II and called for solutions to the problems which were moving us toward world conflict. Later in its history, in the early sixties, the Worker was virtually the first to oppose our entry into the Vietnam War.

It is hard to pinpoint the reason for this ability to forsee the future or the strength to speak out against it. Certainly it proceeds from a vision rooted in faith, but many believers support social policies which Worker people oppose and say "Yes" to a culture, in general, which the Worker does not support. Possibly it is the daily activities Worker people engage in that allow this perception. Being with the poor and the outcast, being in a sense with the victims of our society, discourages any pretense. "Economic upturns" and arms to "stabilize the situation" make little sense here. Being with victims reduces everything to the basics, to life's most harrowing level. Little room is left for illusion.

March 19

Joseph is becoming louder and louder in the afternoon. The past few days he has begun to scream repeatedly, putting his hands over his eyes and yelling "Fire" over and over again. After a few minutes he collapses in tears. Today Joseph had to be taken outside twice and quieted. Steve told me that Joseph had been in a concentration camp in Poland during the war. When he came for his hotel money tonight I put my hand on his shoulder and told him everything would be all right. His face was pale. He took the two dollars, thanked me, and walked out into the night.

March 20

This morning when I walked inside for breakfast Michael and Dorothy were sitting on the patio. Michael was standing up, eating a doughnut and Dorothy, seated on an old chair, was telling him a story. Dorothy called me outside and asked if I would join them. I pulled up a chair. A few minutes later Bruce walked out through the kitchen and took a seat beside us.

Bruce looked good; he had a fresh set of clothes on, his hair was combed, and he had just shaved. Above all, he was sober. Bruce told us that everything was going to change, that later today he was going up to a work camp in the mountains to relax and get his strength back so that he could start life anew. It was the same old story but Bruce is such a lovable person (when he isn't drunk) that you hope against hope that this time he will stay straight. Dorothy told Bruce that he could change his life if he really wanted to. "It takes determination and sacrifice," she said, "but I turned my life around so I know it can be done." When Dorothy spoke these words she looked straight ahead into the kitchen. Her gaze was fixed in the distance. The words were spoken as if her decision to be with the poor was a difficult one, and on the other hand, a fulfillment of her destiny.

Dorothy's conversion had not been an easy one. She had been a part of Greenwich Village life in the early part of the century, which celebrated, among other things, the liberation of the senses. Life was to be lived, experienced to its fullest, free of familial ties and the dictates of bourgeois morality. This was the life she had been immersed in. But with the birth of her child, Tamar, she found a sense of grace that ushered her into the Catholic Church. Her decision to become a Catholic was the putting on of a new life. Many of her old friendships, I am sure, began to dissolve. Her life now was to revolve around the poor and the Church.

The radical stance that she was to take as a Catholic demanded many years of struggle and deprivation. Much of that struggle occurred within the Church she had entered. I often think, when I see her, that the path she chose was never secure or fashionable, and at times must have caused her great pain—certainly, a great deal of sacrifice and prayer.

Meetings with Dorothy are rare for me. Most of the month she stays in a small cottage on Staten Island and when she is here, she spends a great deal of her time in her room on the third floor. When she comes downstairs, it is usually to attend Mass, either here on Monday night, or daily at a church around the corner. She is not young anymore and the noise and the stairs make her weary.

March 21

The United Farm Workers (U.F.W.) is one of the few unionization efforts that the Worker supports wholeheartedly. The support comes because the movement seeks to organize the poorest workers and is arguing as much for the dignity of manual labor as it is for money. Steve, usually before the Friday night meeting, announces a U.F.W. picket line for Saturday. Last week United Farm Workers supporters picketed "Three Brothers Three" a grocery store which sells grapes and iceberg lettuce — two of the items the U.F.W. ask people to boycott. One of the brothers got angry and beat up Steve. His glasses were broken. The leader of the picketline filed a complaint with the police and a charge of assault and battery was leveled against the man. Steve, a non-violent resister of the legal and economic systems in this country was immediately thrown into a dilemma. While the brother had prohibited Steve from speaking the truth as he saw it, Steve sees the legal system as fundamentally violent. After two or three meetings with friends, Steve decided that he would not press charges but would appear before the judge to speak on behalf of the right to picket.

Richard Chavez, the brother of Cesar Chavez who is the leader of the United Farm Workers, spoke last night at the Worker. Thirty or forty people were there including three members of the Socialist Worker Party. Chavez talked about the non-violent struggle to achieve the dignity of labor and the person. At the end of the speech one of the Socialist Worker Party members stood up and talked about the need to confront the system and use violence if necessary. Chavez argued with him and said that it was precisely non-violence which, in the end, would triumph because in that way one freed the oppressors instead of trampling them. Another party member spoke up but the audience drowned out the speaker with applause for Chavez. Though I did not agree with the Socialists I thought of the mob quality of the applause.

March 25

It is 3 A.M. I have just been awakened by the sound of fire engines and the breaking of glass. A building on Second Avenue is on fire. I awoke from a dream startled. In the dream I was lost, wandering through the streets alone and looking for my family. I could not find them. The streets were empty. Under a stoop I saw a man wrapped in newspapers trying to sleep. His face was pale almost as if he were dead. I looked away. When I looked again his face was bloodied. I said to myself that I must go over to the man and comfort him but I could not move my legs. The man screamed and I began to weep. A voice behind me called my name. I turned and saw a shadow disappearing around the corner. I looked back at the man and he was gone. The newspapers were soaked with blood.

March 26

Mater Dolorosa
Mater Dolorosa
Mater Dolorosa,

It was not in the spring among the roses
Or within the walls of the church that claimed
   you
That you appeared.

Mater Dolorosa

You came to me, here, in the nighttime.
When my tears cried out
You held me gently
And did not call me to judgment
Or ask of me things I could not believe.
You would not,
You said you could not
Promise heaven or even the end of this
   loneliness.
No longer the formula deception
Or the mask etched in holiness
Saying only the words
"Be free now to seek your patience."
And then the silence returned.

Mater Dolorosa
Mater Dolorosa
Mater Dolorosa,

How you bore the birth
How you bear both the death and the adoration
I do not know.
I no longer pretend to know your sufferings
Even my own eludes me.
So often the pain is the numbness
The place that is without location or definition,
The underlying, the lying under,

That cannot be touched or altered
Waiting always for the final transformation
    that never comes.

Mater Dolorosa

Under this burden do not turn away.
I will not add, to your weight, my tears.
Desiring only this silence
And the sight of your head bowed in prayer.

March 27

A strange peace has descended on the Worker. There have been no disturbances for two or three days. Jody is being held by the police and Bruce is upstate. Spring is coming. Today the front windows were opened and the fresh air and the afternoon sun added to the tranquility. On days like today there is a certain harmony about being here.

Margaret and Sharon came in for a few minutes and said, "Hello." Ruth and Ralph helped peel potatoes and cut carrots. Sister Nancy cooked dinner. Joseph was quiet, sweeping the floor then cleaning off the tables. After dinner Emily and I went for ice cream to Eleventh Street. We sat at a table, laughing and joking about our life at the Worker. The contrasts between loneliness and laughter here are real.

March 29

We have many dreams,
But like the sun in winter
They remain only warming, fleeting

Like promises unfulfilled, pauses.
And when the dreams are broken
And the winter returns
What shall save us then?
The touching of hands.
A warm embrace.

March 31

Outside my window a car is being hacked to bits by two members of the Hells Angels. The four tires have been slit and now the "angels" are in the process of smashing the car's windows with a lead pipe. Stripped cars are common to the neighborhood. A fully equipped car seen as night falls can be found with nothing but a steering wheel or a rear light in the morning. Everything is taken including the engine. The unusual quality of this demolition is that it takes place in the middle of the day.

Headquarters for the Hells Angels is right down the street. They rent an entire building and display their welcome sign, "Trespassers caught on these premises will be shot on sight." Outside their door they have about twenty motorcycles and an old beat up couch that they sit on and harass passerbys. You literally never know what they will say or do to you as you walk by. I always walk on the other side of the street.

Jason's "house" is on the corner at Ninth Street and Avenue A. It is a wooden shoe shine booth that he has claimed as his own. It is home for him and his large dog. The size of the booth must be about seven feet long and four feet wide. Jason has a heater and comes and goes as he wishes. It is better than a room at a Bowery hotel.

Jason is another person who is so much a part of my life here that he has gone without mention in these pages. Jason is a Southerner in his late thirties, and does odd jobs to scrape money together for his food. He is a familiar face at the Worker usually coming around at nine o'clock at night. At times he is gentle and rational, but often he is brutal with no hint of rationality. Jason is particularly abusive to women and to Margaret especially. A few nights ago he kept three of the volunteers under seige on the first floor till one in the morning. He is too big to hustle out and he is not above throwing chairs at volunteers and overturning tables. As I walk past Ninth Street and see him working on his room though, he says, "Hello" and asks me how everything is going. Often he apologizes for his actions the night before. We never smell whiskey on his breath so none of us know what triggers these rampages. Perhaps it is hunger or simply the frustrations of living the life he does.

April 2

I am now taking the house five times a week. Each shift is five hours long. Beyond that is the soupmeal three hours each day with the person making the soup adding another two hours to his/her work day. Work is so demanding and the time so packed with action that the hours betray the real length of the work day. Rejuvenation appears when a group comes to visit for a week or ten days and works the morning shift. Today five sisters came and plan to stay a week. I was already on the first floor when they came to work so I went down into the basement and sat with the men waiting for the tables to clear. When a group of ten were called from upstairs a scuffle occurred as to who was to be the first to go up. You have to be firm. I told the men to end the argument or they would get no soup. Men seated on the benches echoed my words.

After six months of seeing these men/women each morning I cannot say that I am used to the sight. The sight and smells of cheap wine, worn clothes, and dirt are familiar; their reality has become part of my life. But though the shock has worn off, familiarity has not displaced the despair that fills this basement.

The Bowery person is not simply poor. Poverty denotes an economic reality. Rather, the Bowery person is destitute, stripped of dignity and hope, alive in a desert without an oasis, existing in a world without love or warmth. Often when I sit with these men in the basement my thoughts wander from their scarred and battered faces to the whole of the twentieth century. The twentieth century, after all, has been an age of unparalleled brutality, reducing whole populations to destitution and death. I wonder if the faces in this basement are not simply reflections of our century etched in human flesh.

April 8

Spring has finally arrived. The windows on the first and second floors are open and the house itself feels a little lighter. The main disturbance today is the spring cleaning of Mary's room. Margaret and Emily are cleaning out the objects that Mary has collected over the year. I have been designated to take Mary's collection of clothes over to the clothing room for distribution. The number of bags I have carried over has already reached thirty-five. Mary is not taking this easily. Several people have had to surround her so the cleaning process could go on. She has flown into several rages.

Many of the women on the Bowery are "collectors." The term "shopping bag ladies" is appropriate in this sense. Being homeless, many of the women collect objects and carry them around in bags and carts. Rosienne carries two full shopping carts with her at all times. The bags are full of dishes, knick-knacks, food, clothing, magazines, and hundreds of other items. Perhaps this gives the women a feeling that they are not alone but instead are surrounded by possessions that are personal and their own.

April 11

Renovation of Mary House, where I live, has finally begun. Negotiations with the city and the state took months. Regulations abound: fire doors, so many feet per room, two bathrooms per ten people. The list goes on and on. An architect to draw up the plans, then bids on the work itself. The cost is phenomenal. Most of the regulations are there to protect renters from unscrupulous landlords. But here a community that survives solely on donations is building a home for a group of women for whom the culture and the city have failed to provide. In our society it is costly to serve the poor.

The stairways are being ripped apart, new doorways are being created, old plumbing is being ripped out. Dust is everywhere. Michael sweeps for hours trying to keep the dust down to a minimum but the battle is lost. Tomorrow the wiring is going to be redone so the electricity will be out for a week. Construction crews have been arriving each morning at 7:30 and the noise level is excruciating.

It appears that my new home is being renovated out of existence. For me, it has served its purpose. The last two months have been a time of reflection, a time when I could review my life and my experience here to see what was going on inside of me. Reflection, of course, does not necessarily bring clarity. The volatility of the Worker makes revision of ideas and decisions a necessity of life.

Living with the poor has raised the fundamental question of what being human really means. Does life revolve around one's own fulfillment or is service the basis of life? Can a culture which produces the Lower East Side poor and the Bowery people be judged healthy and supported as is? Do the debates about taxes and welfare consider the fundamental problems of our social system? I think often of what community means now, and what a spiritual affirmation could be. Can we be "religious" and be prosperous in a world filled with the oppressed? I know I cannot change the world but what should I do at least to live out what I believe to be right and just? I suppose each of us takes a lifetime to even approach the answers to these questions. Life here poses them with a sense of urgency.

April 12

Margaret invited me to stay with her for the next couple of weeks because of the conditions over at Mary House. So I am back where I began my stay here, on the roll-away couch, looking out the window and seeing the men standing outside the Worker waiting for soup to be served. The men are again in shirt sleeves and the windows are opened out onto the street. The scene is the same but the differences are many. I have changed considerably and the faces I see are names and persons to me now. For the men, of course, the world remains the same.

I have made two decisions this week. The first is that I shall return to school this fall to study under a professor who is a chronicler of the Worker movement. The second decision is that I will leave here in three weeks. Going back to school will provide me with time to reflect on my experience here in a different environment. Leaving at the end of the month represents a decision that my time here has drawn to a close. It is simply time to go.

When I told Margaret of my decision she gave me a lot of support. To her it was significant that I had stayed this long without a faith commitment. Others had commented that I had been tense and looked tired lately. It is true. I have become obsessed with the difficulties involved for me and have forgotten how hard life is for those I serve.

April 14

Matthew died today. Actually, he died two days ago but his body was discovered today. Jim, worried because Matthew had not come to the Worker for three days, went to his apartment down the street to see if he was all right. Receiving no reply to his knockings on the door, Jim went in through the window. He found Matthew's body slumped in an armchair.

Matthew had lived his entire life in the neighborhood and had been a part of Worker life for years. A lifelong bachelor, he lived simply and was a devoted Catholic. Above all, I think, Matthew was a good person, always with a kind word and a smile. Each day at ten-thirty he would come in, take a bowl of soup and a piece of bread and eat his lunch at a small side table. It was a rare day that Matthew would not mention a book he was reading or toss out an idea for discussion. After lunch he would go down into the basement and think and nap for two or three hours, then come up and help with the setting of the table for dinner. I will always remember Matthew as being gracious and open and deep.

For the last week Matthew had looked very pale and it seemed to me that he was neglecting his appearance and himself. In retrospect I think he had been giving up his life here on earth bit by bit. As he gave up his life, he went deeper and deeper into the mystery of God.

It was strange to see Matthew's chair empty at dinner; no one in the community would sit in his place. The night was rather quiet, and I felt as if something precious had been removed from my life and my work. Later, as dinner was offered to people from the street, a man afflicted with seizures and bleeding from the elbow, sat in Matthew's place. As Steve brought a plate of food to the man, I could not help but wonder about the meaning of life. But with the hectic reality here I knew that Matthew's life and death would soon vanish from my memory. Tonight would be the last time that I would remember his friendly smile as he walked up from the basement to begin helping with dinner.

April 15

The word is out that I am leaving. Comments about the new people who are coming are already circulating. How will they work out knowing nothing about this style of life etc.? I am considered a veteran. The young volunteers will go through the same trials that I went through. How good it feels to be a veteran!

Michael and John told me they were sorry I was leaving but both were excited about my plans for next year. Sitting on the second floor with eight others folding newspapers, I remembered how happy I was when I made my decision to leave. But among people who had, in a strange way, become my friends I could not help but feel a deep sadness about my departure.

Another reason for this sadness is the knowledge that no one is truly missed after a few weeks of absence. New volunteers arrive and they become part of the community. When you tell some people that you are leaving, they simply shrug their shoulders. They have seen hundreds come and go. But though the community's memory may be short, my memory of the community will live on. There are times when I will want to forget this experience, I am sure. That will not be easy to do.

April 16

Living in Margaret's apartment and sleeping on her roll-away couch in the living room necessitates a moving of furniture and making and unmaking the bed twice each day. My clothes are in a suitcase by the couch. I take my showers across the street on the fifth floor. My circumstances are unsettling and impoverished. So in one sense I am really living in voluntary poverty. Still I retain my desire to collect material goods; books, the fifty or so dollars I have and my writings. For the last three months my clothing has come out of the clothing room like everyone else's. Yet I still cannot stand being dirty. In short, I want my poverty to be pristine and informed; a deprivation with culture. As you give up more and more you realize that the few things you carry with you can become more and more burdensome. However, no matter how much you give up, you fight to remain different from the people you serve. To a remark by a construction worker working at Mary House, that I was unemployed and being helped by the Worker, I immediately "straightened him out," by telling him I was helping others and not being helped. My remark was hardly accurate but the point is that for personal survival I felt it necessary to maintain the difference between the volunteers (myself) and the Bowery people or the poor. I need to assure myself, as my friends and family need to be assured, that I am in the midst of "this" world but have not entered it.

April 20

I am no longer taking the house. The last few days I have been free to visit with people on the second floor. In the afternoons I have been taking walks and just generally relaxing. Last night John took me out for an ice cream. Finally, instead of being asked to contribute, I have been awarded money from the Bishops Relief Fund! John is usually kidding around but tonight he was serious. He talked about the Church and about the Worker itself. Very often a person like John can correct the surface impressions one gets from being here a few months. Where I saw a great amount of violence during my stay, John can talk from twenty years' experience and put my stay in perspective. He says that the violence comes in cycles, sometimes lasting for months, sometimes quieting down for a year. But over the years the violence has become worse. Drugs and the employment situation are two of the reasons.

When we returned from our ice cream John went upstairs to bed and I came down to the first floor to see who had the house. It turned out that Margaret was filling in for Sharon. Alex was asleep in a chair and the room was quiet. She asked me if I had decided what transportation I was going to take when I left for home. I told her the bus. She was answering letters; I went up to the second floor to see what was on television. Louis was watching a Western. As I went downstairs intent on going to bed, I saw Perkins in the hallway as drunk as I have ever seen him. Margaret asked if I would take him to a Bowery hotel. Perkins looked up at me as if to say "please" but instead started to fall over. Trying to get Perkins to a Bowery hotel when he is this drunk is no easy task. He does not want you to touch him, but he is constantly on the brink of falling into oncoming traffic. There is an art to walking him home, knowing when he is just rocking back and forth, and when, in fact, he is going to fall. It is only three blocks away and the walk invariably takes a half an hour.

April 25

Jim left this evening and I will leave next week. After working with Jim for eight months I cannot say that I knew him very well. Even when we were both living on the fifth floor he kept completely to himself. Sharon accompanied him to the bus station; the rest of us said goodbye on the first floor. I shook his hand and wished him good luck. Perkins gave him a hug and Jim promised to keep in touch.

May 2

I will leave tomorrow with mixed feelings. On the one hand, there is a feeling of strength that I have survived the year and I chose to leave at the right time, and on the other hand, a feeling of sadness that my stay here is ending. It has been a long journey for me, one might even say a painful journey if I had not received so much in return.

It has been a time of questioning, a time when everything, every belief and understanding no matter how informed and profound, has been turned upside down and around. It is hard to know where I will land.

Instead of philosophy or the intellect, the experience itself has raised the fundamental questions of commitment and service. The poor and the destitute are no longer invisible or far away. They are before me and within me.

The answers are less clear. Certainly a desire for a vision of a new society has been irrevocably planted inside of me. Perhaps we all have a yearning for the new society deep inside of us. Often, out of fear, we step away. Perhaps the great paradox is that the nurturance of this vision comes from the place we least expect, the hard place as well as the place of numbness. For me this seed has been planted among those who seem, at first glance, and in the eyes of the world, to be so sterile. It may be that by serving these suffering ones we witness our own complicity. It may simply be a mystery. "The stone which the builders have rejected, has become the cornerstone."

I have heard of people who have left the Worker becoming bitter and angry with the world. Some have become cynical. Ugliness and brutality are not easy to witness and remain whole. The Worker has always been the announcer of the new society rather than the denouncer of the old. "Build a new society within the shell of the old." Only this forceful and suffering love has kept a longing for a new world from sinking into despair. I must remember to love.

T. S. Eliot wrote about the rose garden where existence and eternity, dream and finality met in the spring. A garden, he envisioned, of peace and perfection where all suffering was transformed into beatitude. The roses, now without thorns, surrounded the garment of the Lady and greeted the announcing angel. "He comes to set captives free." While it is true that the meeting of the Lady and the angel eludes me, I now know who tends the garden.

Epilogue

My departure from the Worker demanded of me as much reflection as my arrival. Ralph, who was almost always in need of money, pressed ten dollars into my hand "for a special treat on the bus." He would not take "no" for an answer. I had found out the night before that the bus ride was to be thirty-six hours long, and Sister Nancy joked about the journey I had ahead of me. Joan apologized for her "silly" remarks concerning my reasons for being at the Worker. I shook hands with Steve. When I said good-bye to Louis, a man who, despite his strange ways, I had come to respect, he turned away and pretended not to notice. Christine refused to speak to me. Michael hugged me and wished me well. Sharon offered to accompany me to the bus station. Sister Ann said farewell on the subway platform. As the train entered the station we embraced. She began to weep. Quickly she turned and ran up the stairs. We had grown close during the year but somehow the tears were unexpected. Inside the train I stood looking across at Sharon wondering what, if anything, I could say. It has been three years since that day but the memory remains vivid.

I had never been "comfortable" at the Worker. My year had been characterized by anxiety and a sense of trial. The marks and smells of the destitute permeated the basement and it remained as ominous when empty in the late afternoon as it was terrifying when the benches were filled in the morning. The first floor abounded with those whom life had broken, old and young alike. The sagging beds and transient bodies on the fifth floor made it apparent that this should never be a home for anyone. Rarely was there a time when the cries of the wounded were not to be heard. "The whole world is a hospital," Eliot wrote years ago. In their affliction I began to recognize my own affliction. The Bowery people as well as the poor of the Lower East Side were no different than I except in circumstance. We are all in need of care and love. Our condition is common. This was the most difficult lesson I was to learn from my year at the Worker.

I also began to question in deeper ways the basic structures of our society. What are the consequences of our social and economic systems? Certainly they are far more than deprivation of material goods. What does living in large metropolitan areas do to people, especially to the poor? Why are so many being left behind and abandoned? Why are there so many wounded?

To me it seems that the fundamental question of our lives, and perhaps of our century, is not the discovery of new knowledge or the development of new technology, but whether or not we can commit ourselves as persons and as a society to love and serve each other. Can we, amidst the ideologies and perplexities of our age, rediscover the human face and soul?

The Catholic Worker has continued over the years to believe in the transforming power of love and service. It has done so during the purges in the

139

Soviet Union, the death camps in Nazi Germany, and the war in Viet Nam. To some, perhaps even to a majority, this vision of transforming love, drawn amidst the background of hatred and violence, seems simplistic and romantic. Indeed the world has chosen other paths to travel. For forty-five years however, the Catholic Worker has offered its vision of a more human society. After having witnessed the transformation myself I know I can never dismiss this vision of love.

Interview with the Author—1999

Oral History Memoir

Baylor University Institute for Oral History

Interviewee: Marc H. Ellis
Date: 20 October 1999
Place: Institute for Oral History, Baylor University
Interviewer: Greg Garrett

GREG GARRETT: Tell us about your upbringing and education and give us a little bit of background about your family life.

MARC ELLIS: I was born in North Miami Beach, Florida, in 1952 in a transplanted Jewish New York neighborhood. My parents had come down to Miami Beach independent of each other with their families at a very young age. My father has been in Miami Beach since the 1930s and my mother as well. I am native Floridian. I grew up in North Miami Beach, went to a public school, but also went to Hebrew School. I started out at an Orthodox synagogue because our area was new and there were no conservative or reform synagogues. When the conservative synagogue was built I went there and was trained there and became a Bar Mitzvah.

In my schooling I was in two different worlds. One was America. I was taught in elementary school and beyond mostly, except for one exception, by people who were not Jewish. I didn't really know what they were. Looking back now some of them were Southern in culture, probably Christian, but I could not identify too much where they were from. In our public schooling, Jews weren't really mentioned. In Hebrew School, growing up in the 1950s, the Holocaust was present although not yet named. It was in the background. Some of my teachers were from Europe. I also had a teacher from Israel. She had been born in Europe, gone to Israel, and then come to the States.

It was like being in two worlds. I was learning Hebrew, which was a very foreign language to me. My native language was English. I heard stories about the prophets and the Bible on the one hand, and on the other hand was assimilating into American life. It was like being in two different worlds.

My parents were trying to hold these worlds together. We were lower middle class. My father was an insurance salesman and later a greeting card salesman. My mother went back to school and became a teacher, ultimately achieving her Ph.D. She was part of the first generation of women who went back to school. And so I had a greeting card salesman as a father, not educated in any significant way, never went to college or went for a semester and didn't do well, and my mother, who was going back to college and was very bright in that way. They sent us to Hebrew School and we observed the holidays, especially Hanukah and Passover. So it was neither a deeply religious family nor a secular family. I believe most Jews of my generation in the United States grew up pretty much that way.

GARRETT: Then you went off to college.

ELLIS: I went to Florida State University. I was accepted to American University. I was very attracted to that university because President Kennedy had given his famous foreign policy speech there. I was a big fan of Kennedy and a supporter of civil rights. I was accepted there and given some money but it just wasn't enough. We couldn't afford the expenses. Although my parents said they would send me, I felt it was too much so I had to go in-state, or felt I had to, and I decided to go to a university where none of my friends were going. I wanted something different and most of my friends were going to the University of Florida or the University of South Florida. I went to Florida State University. I'm very glad I did because it was there that I happened into a Religious Studies class with Bill Swain. In that class I was introduced to Martin Buber. I had never read anything like Buber, to put it mildly. We read *I and Thou* and Dr. Swain made tapes for people to listen to and to further their knowledge of Buber. I used to go into the library and listen to these big-reel tapes for hours on end.

So it was there I was able to enter religiosity through English in a university environment. It was in that class, too, that I encountered Asian religions, which I knew very little. I discovered Zen—or parts of Zen—that later would become important to me. I also encountered Black and feminist theology. We read James Cone and I met Rosemary Ruether during that time. In the spring of my freshman year I listened to a lecture by Richard Rubenstein. He is the author of *After Auschwitz* and many other books. I took several courses with him. It was during that time that the naming of the Holocaust was taking place and he was one of the people naming this horrific event. I landed there and from that moment on I had a double major in Sociology and Religious Studies, but my focus was religious studies because the professors were asking questions of meaning and significance. I was very much drawn to that.

GARRETT: How would you describe Rubenstein's influence on your life and work?

ELLIS: Profound. It's not that I've had an intimate friendship with Rubenstein, none at all. But the questions he posed were so stark, about the brokeness of the covenant and the brokeness of human history. They were also compelling. It is these questions and the other parts of religiosity I was learning about, with my background from Hebrew School and with my meeting with William Miller later in my undergraduate days, that sent me to the Catholic Worker. I would say I was formed religiously at Florida State University. So that department was very instrumental, and Rubenstein especially, because of the starkness of his questions.

GARRETT: Was it also at university that you began to confront Christianity?

ELLIS: Yes. I didn't know anything about Christianity. We had one Christian on the block who was called a Gentile of German background. My father had a few prejudices about him. I saw the Christian trappings of our culture, especially in the department stores and shopping centers around Christmas time. But I couldn't have told you the difference between a Roman Catholic and a Protestant. I was unaware of denominations. I could not have named one of them. And as far as I can recall, I had never been inside a church. So when I went to Florida State, the discussion in religious studies involved many things: aspects of Judaism that I didn't know about, but also Christianity and Asian religions. People talked about them as if I could readily enter into the discussion. In fact I knew little. I just started learning. I had a girlfriend who was an Episcopalian and I went with her several times to church. It was the first time I entered a church.

GARRETT: What was it that led you to work with the Catholic Worker?

ELLIS: Well, with Rubenstein, I had come to a dead end. I didn't know what the answers were to his questions, but I also realized that his answers couldn't be my answers. In my senior year, I met William Miller through a series of bag lunches on the Catholic Worker. I hadn't heard of the Catholic Worker, but one of my teachers suggested that I might be interested and I attended the brown bag series. What Miller had done was to tape interviews of people at the Catholic Worker. They were, to me at least, very strange interviews with people on the street and people who had volunteered and lived at the Catholic Worker. What interested me about Miller was he didn't say anything. He just played the tapes. I became very interested in him. He was very humble about things and did not inter-ject much. After getting to know him a bit, if he saw me walking he would just ask me if I want-ed to go for a ride or come out to the house. He would pick me up and we just started talking. He had written a book on Dorothy Day titled *A Harsh and Dreadful Love: Dorothy Day and The Catholic Worker Movement.* It is a beautiful book. Again, it was still very foreign. It contained vari-ous levels of the Catholic tradition that I was learning about from Lawrence Cunningham, also a professor in the Religious Studies department.

In my senior year Dorothy Day came to visit Miller. I met her. I had been very much into Camus, which I probably picked up from Rubenstein's interest in him. And I asked her—in retrospect it seems like a stupid question, but Camus asked it and it wasn't sophomoric when he asked it—I asked her if you could be a saint without God. Dorothy was already in her seventies. She was still able to address a group but I remember her being confused and not really answering the question. Then I read *A Harsh and Dreadful Love*. I went home for the summer. I had applied to Vanderbilt for a master's program, received recommendations from people like Rubenstein, and was accepted with a scholarship. And then I decided that I would not go to Vanderbilt. I remember it was at Florida State in the spring that I mailed that letter saying that I was not going. I knew it would change my life because from Vanderbilt I would have gone to Harvard. Instead of going to Vanderbilt, I went to the Catholic Worker in New York City. I had just finished Dostoevsky's *Crime and Punishment*. I was very taken by the characters in the novel and went up to the Catholic Worker and began to live and work there.

GARRETT: What had you learned about Dorothy Day that inspired that kind of impulsive action?

ELLIS: This was in the heyday of the Catholic Worker. That was the post-Vatican II period. You had the peace movement around Vietnam, at which the Catholic Worker had been very much in the forefront. You had questions not only about pacifism but about justice, about the poor, about building a society that was just and good. You had all of these questions in the Catholic community that had gone through Vatican II. It was a very beautiful community and people used to come one after another to meet Dorothy Day. She was a saint of this movement. She hated to be called a saint and I even saw some people drop to their knees in front of her. She would get very upset and tell them to get up off their knees.

I don't want to pretend that I was a friend of Dorothy Day. I lived at the Catholic Worker in the same building. I had lunch with her and dinner with her, and we had several chats, but I never wanted to pretend an easy familiarity. She was physically beautiful, a woman in her seventies, who radiated beauty. Obviously it wasn't just physical, but when you looked at her you just saw this beauty. She lived with other women who were poor. She was quite clean and had a manner of living which was very much apart, yet she lived with others. She was strong. She could get angry. She was ferocious. And yet humble.

One time I had responsibility for the house, which meant that I was the person responsible for who came in and out of the building. Sometimes you would have to toss people out if they became abusive or violent. People you had to toss out could probably beat you to a pulp, so you had to learn how to do this and I did, which amazed me. I used to take these big guys who were drunk. You learned how to negotiate with them and then usher them out. On Christmas Day—and this was one of my most vivid memories of her—Dorothy was downstairs. She didn't come down all the time because it was too difficult negotiating the stairs. She was peeling potatoes for the soup because she hated potatoes in the soup that weren't peeled. And this man came in, who was really nice when he wasn't drunk but he was awful when he was, and he started cussing her and everybody else out. It was Christmas Day and I had the house and I said "Henry, this can't happen on Christmas." He proceeded to punch me and knee me in the groin. As I bent over, he got me in a headlock where I couldn't breathe. I thought I was dying. Henry was strong and he was possessed. Anyway, finally I broke free, or he let me free, and I remember staggering back to my seat next to Dorothy. I was confused about where I was. Dorothy leaned over and said very quietly, "I was praying for you Marc."

Another incident: I went away for the Easter vacation with a person at the Worker who had brought me to her home. When I came back, Dorothy was coming down the stairs. I walked in, and she said, "Oh Marc, it's so good to have you back." Dorothy had the habit of kissing on the lips, a chaste kiss, but in our home we always kissed on the cheek. She came toward me and I said to myself, "Oh my God, Dorothy Day is going to kiss me on the lips," and she did.

GARRETT: At what point during your experience there did you realize that you wanted to write something about it?

ELLIS: Well, I had been writing for some time, not with any idea of a publication. I wrote poetry as a young person and I had taken to writing diaries. I don't mean sophisticated, elaborate schedules. I would write down reflections and write quotes from what I had been reading. While there I jotted down some aspects of my experience, so what became *A Year at the Catholic*

Worker was really just diaries and poetry that I wrote with no thought that it would ever be published.

William Miller used to come up and visit Dorothy in New York because he wanted to write her biography. She did not want it written while she was alive because there were aspects of her life before her conversion that were, at least to her mind, scandalous. He used to come and visit her, talking about things she had done, and he used to visit me too. At first, he was surprised to see me there and wanted to bring me back. At the end of the year, I went back to Florida State to do a master's program with him. He said, "Just go to the library, read and write," which is what I did. And when it came to thesis time, and I asked him what I should do as my thesis, he had been aware that I had written some diaries and said "Why don't you write them up?" I said "Dr. Miller, that is not a scholarly work!" He said "You do that." It became quite a controversy at Florida State from people in other departments who saw me as going on to the Ivy League and who wondered whether that kind of writing would help me accomplish that goal.

GARRETT: In writing the thesis, how did you work with Miller? Did he have a role in shaping it?

ELLIS: Miller didn't shape anything. I just wrote them up and handed them to him. I don't think he marked one line. He just would sit there and say, "Marc, that's good." I was completely free. That was Miller's style and temperament. But what he read, that's not the whole book. That was half. When I went to New Orleans the following year, I had a few mimeographed copies, and people asked me where I had been and about my writing. I said the Catholic Worker. They read my thesis and liked it. And that's when I got the idea that it might be something to publish. I thought that maybe a Catholic press would be interested in it, but I really had no idea; I'd never sent anything off to be published anywhere. So I went to a library at a local Catholic college in New Orleans and looked through the periodicals. I thought that it would be the size of an article. I still hadn't thought of a book. I pulled ten periodicals off the shelf and the first one was *New Catholic World,* which is a Catholic magazine that began publishing in the 1800s. I sent it off to them. It turns out that *New Catholic World* is published by Paulist Press. I received a letter back from an editor at both, *New Catholic World* and Paulist Press, Robert Hyer, saying that it was too long for an article and too short for a book. Would I expand it and they would publish it as a book? That is what I did.

GARRETT: What sort of editorial help did you get from them?

ELLIS: None. In fact, I can't remember them sending it back for work at all. I expanded it, maybe doubled it in size or more, and sent it back. By the way, Hyer said he knew it was good because he gave it to his secretary and she loved it.

GARRETT: Did you know that it was good?

ELLIS: Well, when I was writing it I wasn't even

thinking of it. And when people started telling me that it was interesting, I thought "Well, it probably is; I don't know." I wasn't thinking about it, but when it came out it was reviewed in many places and received very good reviews. In fact, every review was good. So I didn't think about it that much but, yes, I knew it was important to me. I thought that it was a way for me to express myself. That's when I began to think of myself as a writer.

GARRETT: Tell us a little bit about where you went from the time you finished the book and it was published to your later preparations to your later academic positions.

ELLIS: When I left New Orleans, I went up to Milwaukee where Miller was then teaching at Marquette University. I had a big suitcase full of books, clothes, and I didn't know what I was going to do. I stayed with him. He always welcomed me and others into his home, and one day—it was late August early September—I said, "Dr. Miller, I don't know what I'm going to do." He said, "Why don't you get a Ph.D.?" I said, "In what?" He said, "In the history of ideas, in religion." I said, "Okay, where should I do it?" He said, "Why don't you just do it with me?" And I said, "Well it's September already. I'll have to apply and then wait a year or so." He said, "No, you'll start tomorrow." And he went down and arranged a full fellowship and I started. That's how I went. I never applied. I never filled out an application for a master's degree or the Ph.D. I spent three years at Marquette.

In the meantime, while Dorothy was alive she forbade Miller from writing her biography and instructed him to write the biography of Peter Maurin who had founded the Catholic Worker with her. One day I asked him how the Peter Maurin book was coming. Miller replied that he wasn't writing it anymore. He had stopped. I said, "If you don't do it, who will?" Miller answered, "You will." The papers of Dorothy Day and Peter Maurin were given to the Marquette archives and that's where I did my dissertation, which I wrote as a book. It was published with the title, *Peter Maurin: Prophet in the Twentieth Century*.

As I was finishing up at Marquette, thinking about what I was going to do next, I received a letter from a Maryknoll priest who was on the governing board of their religious community. He had picked up a copy of *A Year at the Catholic Worker* in a New York bookstore and had written my publishers a letter in which he related his experience among the poor in Bolivia with my experience among the poor in New York City. I received the letter as I was beginning to look through job possibilities and not seeing anything of interest (and I don't know that any of them would have been interested in me). I asked my friends about Maryknoll and missionaries. Missionaries were not a favorite topic in my home. But people suggested that I might be interested and I wrote and asked them if they had something for me. I told them that I'd like to teach people who are committed to the poor:

"You seem to be doing that. Do you have a school? Do you have anything for me?" They didn't respond on specifics but asked me to fly to New York. The first day there I was hired to teach in their school of theology.

And that is where I stayed untill 1995, when they closed the school. I was off at Harvard for a few years and in between I went to Florida State for a year or so as a visiting professor replacing Richard Rubenstein who had retired. Ultimately, then, I came to Baylor. The Maryknoll experience was heavily involved in liberation theology which, in many ways, is an extension of Catholic Worker understandings brought up to date and in a Third World context.

GARRETT: So you see logical extensions from the Catholic Worker experience to what you've done since?

ELLIS: Yes, although I was a terrible Catholic Worker. I always say I was the worst Catholic Worker in history, because it was very difficult for me to see suffering up close. It was a very difficult and rewarding experience, but in retrospect I would say that I was a failure. Nonetheless, it is one of the foundations of my life. It introduced me to a world of thinkers and theologians and activists that I either didn't know existed or only dimly knew existed. I learned about them in a place of activity on behalf of justice. It brought them to life.

When I went to the Worker, I didn't go because it was Catholic. I went because it proposed to me the possibility of commitment and I thought that was the response to Rubenstein's questions about God and the covenant and the breaking of all solidarity including solidarity with human beings. That commitment was the response that could help me deal with those questions in a way that was fruitful for me. Maryknoll represented that also for me. It also broadened my horizons because I traveled all over the world with Maryknoll and I directed a justice and peace master's program there. I encountered a world of struggling peoples, a world of diverse Christianities, and methods of doing theology. Mixed together, the Catholic Worker, Maryknoll, my Jewishness, . . . it brought me to another level of spirituality awareness.

GARRETT: Do you see your interest in justice for the Palestinians as being just another aspect of this concern for the downtrodden that comes out in your life from that time to this?

ELLIS: Yes, although it has a more specific Jewish dimension. My ability to meet Palestinians and cross the boundary of Jew and Palestinian is, to some extent, like crossing the boundary to meet someone who is poor in our culture. You recognize that the primary difference is not power or poverty. We are involved in a system that is denying a community's humanity. Here, I come more as a Jew and ask not only what is my responsibility as a human being, which is a big question, but also what is my responsibility as a Jew. In *A Year at the Catholic Worker* I was Jewish, obviously, and I was asking some of those questions in a much broader framework, which is not to say that asking them in a Jewish way is less broad. It is a different framework. When you ask about the connection, I would say sure, it's remembering being at the Catholic Worker, sitting in the basement when we had so many people on the soup line and I would regulate the flow of how they came up. I remember the smells in the basement, the violence in the basement and some of the resignation in the basement. I have seen those faces in different ways everywhere in the world.

GARRETT: Do you think that because you've spent the majority of your adult life in the company of Christians and in Christian institutions that it's enriched you more than if you had spent it among fellow Jews?

ELLIS: I realized at a very young age that I could not find out what it meant to be Jewish only in the Jewish community. Now, the journey among Christians really happened unplanned, step by step. It just happened. But I had questions about Christianity—and I wanted to find out for myself. Were Christians always going to be like the Christians I had read about in Europe or were they changing? I wanted to know that. I had a deep need to know what this Christianity was really about and I wanted to know for myself. And after that I began to realize that I could learn from Christians. I mean I have had a battle with Christianity, coming from my background, but also an opening with Christians who are critical about their history and are open about religious questions. The experience of Christianity has been deeply enriching at many, many levels and forced me to think through my Jewishness at another level.

GARRETT: As you look back on *A Year at the Catholic Worker* now, from a space of some years, how do you look at it both as a writer and as a theologian? Is it something that you're proud of?

ELLIS: Yes. The Catholic Worker is a young Marc, but it also may be the truest Marc. I don't often reread parts of the book, but when I do I feel that experience is still very important to me. I never think of whether I am proud of any book I write. I don't think of it that way but rather does it express a part of my own journey. I am very pleased and moved that it is being reprinted. It is like bringing back a part of my life into the public realm.

GARRETT: In the years since you first wrote *A Year at the Catholic Worker,* you have been extremely prolific both as a writer and as a speaker. For those who are coming to your work for the first time, I wonder if you could sum up what you feel are the main strains of thought that you have been exploring for the past twenty years in your other published work.

ELLIS: In one way, it is all here in *A Year at the Catholic Worker.* I have traveled and learned a lot in the past years. But the questions about God, loneliness, solidarity, the questions of beauty and tragedy are all here. I have continued to explore those themes. I see *A Year at the Catholic Worker* and my other writings as a continuity. *A Year at the Catholic Worker* is the initial raising of

the questions. I also think that I have come closer to the embrace that I sought at the Catholic
Worker in areas of my life. It is like being in a
dark room where you light certain candles to see,
and one of them, the Catholic Worker, is still
burning.

Selected Bibliography

Books

A Year at the Catholic Worker (New York: Paulist Press, 1978); reprinted under the title *A Year at the Catholic Worker: A Spiritual Journey Among the Poor* (Waco, TX: Baylor University Press, 2000).

Peter Maurin: Prophet in the Twentieth Century (New York: Paulist Press, 1981).

Faithfulness in the Age of Holocaust (Amity, NY: Amity House, 1986).

Toward a Jewish Theology of Liberation (Maryknoll, NY: Orbis Books, 1987, 1989).

Beyond Innocence and Redemption: Confronting the Holocaust and Israeli Power (San Francisco: Harper and Row, 1990).

The Renewal of Palestine in the Jewish Imagination (London: Alhani International Books, Ltd., 1994).

Ending Auschwitz: The Future of Jewish and

162

Christian Life (Louisville, KY: Westminster/John Knox Press, 1994).

Unholy Alliance: Religion and Atrocity in Our Time (Minneapolis, MN: Fortress Press, 1997).

O Jerusalem!: The Contested Future of the Jewish Covenant (Minneapolis, MN: Fortress Press, 1999).

Revolutionary Forgiveness: A Jewish Journey Among Christians (Waco, TX: Baylor University Press, forthcoming).

Co-Edited Books

(w/Otto Maduro) *The Future of Liberation Theology: Essays in Honor of Gustavo Gutiérrez* (Maryknoll, NY: Orbis Books, 1989).

(w/Rosemary Radford Ruether) *Beyond Occupation: American Jewish, Christian, and Palestinian Voices for Peace* (Boston: Beacon Press, 1990).

(w/Otto Maduro) *Expanding the View: Gustavo Gutiérrez and the Future of Liberation Theology* (Maryknoll, NY: Orbis Books, 1990).

(w/Naim Stifan Ateek and Rosemary Radford Ruether) *Faith and the Intifada: Palestinian*

Christian Voices (Maryknoll, NY: Orbis Books, 1992).

(w/Daniel A. McGowan) *Remembering Deir Yassin: The Future of Israel and Palestine* (New York: Olive Branch Press, 1998).

Articles and Book Chapters

Marc H. Ellis's many articles have appeared in diverse American and international journals including *International Herald Tribune* (Paris), *European Judaism* (London), *New Outlook* (Tel Aviv), *Jordan Times* (Jordan), *Ecumenical Review* (Geneva), *Common Ground* (Korea), *Ord & Bild* (Sweden), *Christian Century* (Chicago), and *Journal of Palestine Studies* (Washington, D.C.).

His essays have been published in a number of anthologies, most recently in *Contemporary Jewish Theology: A Reader*, edited by Elliot Dorff and Luis Newman (New York: Oxford University Press, 1998).